Health for Life

Authors
Julius B. Richmond
John D. MacArthur Professor of
Health Policy
Director, Division of Health Policy
Research and Education
Harvard University
Advisor on Child Health Policy
Children's Hospital of Boston
Boston, Massachusetts

Elenore T. Pounds
Health Education Writer
Downers Grove, Illinois

Physical Fitness Author
Charles B. Corbin
Professor, Department of Health
and Physical Education
Arizona State University
Tempe, Arizona

Scott, Foresman and Company
Editorial Offices: Glenview, Illinois

Regional Offices: Sunnyvale, California •
Tucker, Georgia • Glenview, Illinois •
Oakland, New Jersey • Dallas, Texas

Authors

Julius B. Richmond, M.D., is the John D. MacArthur Professor of Health Policy and the Director of the Division of Health Policy Research and Education at Harvard University. He also is Advisor on Child Health Policy at the Children's Hospital of Boston. Dr. Richmond served as Surgeon General for the U.S. Public Health Service and as Assistant Secretary for Health from 1977–1981. Trained as a pediatrician, Dr. Richmond joined the faculty of the Harvard Medical School in 1971. He was professor of child psychiatry and human development before being appointed Surgeon General.

Elenore T. Pounds, M.A., is a health education writer and lecturer. A former elementary teacher, she served as directing editor of the Health and Personal Development Program. She is co-author of *Health and Growth, You and Your Health,* and other health publications.

Charles B. Corbin, Ph.D., is professor and coordinator of graduate studies in the Department of Health and Physical Education at Arizona State University. A former elementary physical education teacher, he previously served as professor and head of graduate studies in the Department of Health, Physical Education, and Recreation at Kansas State University. Dr. Corbin is the author of many research and professional publications, especially in the area of lifetime fitness.

ISBN: 0-673-29503-6

2345678910RRW959493929190898887

Consultants

Reading
Robert A. Pavlik, Ed.D.
Professor and Chairperson
Reading–Language Arts Department
Cardinal Stritch College
Milwaukee, Wisconsin

Medical
Jerry Newton, M.D.
Director, Health Services
San Antonio Independent School District
Clinical Professor, Pediatrics
University of Texas Medical School, San Antonio
San Antonio, Texas

Design
Design direction by Norman Perman
Graphic Designer and Art Consultant
Chicago, Illinois

Cover photograph by Ralph Cowan

Acknowledgments
The dental health information contained in Chapter 4 is considered by the American Dental Association to be in accord with current scientific knowledge, 1986.

For further acknowledgments, see page 220.

Content Specialists

Dental Health
Mary Banas
Program Specialist
Bureau of Health Education and Audiovisual Services
American Dental Association
Chicago, Illinois

Drug Education
Chwee Lye Chng
Assistant Professor
Division of Health Education
North Texas State University
Denton, Texas

Nutrition
Jean Mayer
President
Tufts University
Medford, Massachusetts

Safety and First Aid
Janice Sutkus
Technical Specialist
National Safety Council
Chicago, Illinois

Reviewers and Contributors

Lourdes Alcorta-Rogover
Educational Consultant
Former Teacher
Miami, Florida

Ruth Ann Althaus
Professor of Public Health
Master of Public Health Program
Illinois Benedictine College
Lisle, Illinois

Matthew Bustamante
Bilingual/Cross-Cultural Education Specialist
Bandini Elementary School
Montebello, California

Judi Coffey
Educational Consultant
Learning Disabilities Specialist
Jonesboro, Arkansas

Bryan Cooke
Professor
Department of Community Health
College of Health and Human Services
University of Northern Colorado
Greeley, Colorado

Gail Daud
Teacher in Gifted Education
Spring Shadows Elementary School
Houston, Texas

Bo Fernhall
Director, Fitness and Cardiac Rehabilitation
Department of Physical Education
Northern Illinois University
DeKalb, Illinois

Linda Froschauer
Teacher
Weston Public Schools
Weston, Connecticut

Rosalyn Gantt
Teacher
Midway Elementary School
Cincinnati, Ohio

Jon Hisgen
School Health Coordinator
Pewaukee Public Schools
Pewaukee, Wisconsin

Peter Loudis
Teacher of Gifted and Talented
Spring Branch Junior High School
Houston, Texas

Jeanne Mannings
Teacher
Adamsville Elementary School
Atlanta, Georgia

Wanda Nottingham-Brooks
Learning Disabilities Teacher
Morrisonville Junior and Senior High School
Morrisonville, Illinois

Bert Pearlman
Director, Curriculum Research and Evaluation
Office of the County Superintendent of Schools
Santa Barbara, California

Candace Purdy
Health Teacher
Maine South High School
Park Ridge, Illinois

Joan Salmon
School Nurse
Greenwood School Corporation
Greenwood, Indiana

David R. Stronck
Associate Professor of Health Education
Department of Teacher Education
California State University, Hayward
Hayward, California

Merita Thompson
Professor
Department of Health Education
Eastern Kentucky University
Richmond, Kentucky

Shirley Van Sickle
Health Teacher
DeVeaux Junior High School
Toledo, Ohio

Chapter 1 You and Your Feelings 16

Chapter 2 Food and Your Health 38

Chapter 3 You and Your Body 66

Chapter 4 Caring For Your Teeth 92

Chapter 5 You and Your Safety 120

Chapter 6 Medicines, Drugs, and Your Health 148

Chapter 7 Your Physical Fitness 172

Chapter 8 A Healthy Community 198

Why Learn About Health

"When you have your health, you have just about everything." You might have heard this saying before. What does it mean to you? Most people agree that good health is one of the most important things a person could have. When you are healthy, you can enjoy life more fully. Good health helps you think clearly and get along with others at school. Good health keeps your body working properly so you can enjoy your play. Good health helps you look and feel your best.

Learning about health is important because you are making more and more decisions about your own health. For example, you might decide what to eat for lunch or where to play after school.

To make the wisest decisions, you need good information. Then you need to know how to use this information. Scott, Foresman's *Health for Life* has the information that can improve your health, but it is up to you to use it. Make good health a part of your day and a part of your life, now and in the years to come.

When You Read This Book

1. Read the question.

2. Look at the pictures.

3. Find the answer.

1 Who Is Most Responsible for Keeping You Safe?

Suppose you were waiting to cross the street as this girl is doing. What would you do before crossing? What is the safe way to be sure you cross after all cars have stopped?

The girl knows that she is responsible for keeping herself safe. She is following a safety rule that she has learned. She always waits on the curb and looks left, right, and then left again before crossing any street. Following this rule helps keep her safe.

Just like this girl, you are responsible for keeping yourself safe. Other people can only help keep you safe. You are most responsible for your own safety. Following safety rules can help keep you safe.

This girl looks to the left, right, and then left again to keep herself safe.

4. Learn the health word.

Being careful can help keep you safe. For example, you can help prevent an **injury** when you watch where you walk on stairs. You do not want to fall and hurt yourself. Hold on to a railing if possible.

injury (in′jər ē), damage to the body.

Thinking of ways to prevent accidents can also help keep you safe. Suppose you and your friends want to play ball in the park. Before you play, you should carefully check the playing field for sharp objects. How might this rule help prevent injuries?

Think back • *Study on your own with Study Guide page 230.*

1. Who is most responsible for your safety?
2. What can help a person be a safe walker?
3. What can a person do to help prevent accidents?

5. Use what you learned.

Chapter 1

You and Your Feelings

What different feelings does this girl have? You have different feelings too. Sometimes you feel one way. Sometimes you feel another way. Your feelings are a part of you.

The lessons in this chapter tell about the different feelings that people have. You will learn what to do about feelings that trouble you. You will also learn how to get along with others. Knowing how to get along with others can help you feel happy now and in the future.

feelings, the way a person feels about something.

1 How Do You and Others Show Feelings?

On Your Own
Each child in the picture feels differently about the rainstorm that spoiled their picnic. Write a paragraph explaining why each child feels as he or she does.

Sometimes you might feel happy or sad or angry. Sometimes you might feel worried or disappointed or surprised. Happiness, sadness, anger, worry, and surprise are **feelings.** You have feelings and so does everyone else.

Sometimes faces show how people feel. Look at the children's faces shown here. It rained just as they were going on a picnic. How do you think each child feels about the rainstorm?

Sometimes voices show how people feel. Bill said in an angry voice, "Why did it rain and spoil our picnic?" Can you make your voice sound angry like Bill's voice?

Sometimes people show feelings in the way they stand or move. Look again at the children in the pictures. Does the way each is standing help show his or her feelings? How might someone who feels proud walk?

Think Back • *Study on your own with Study Guide page 222.*

1. What are some feelings people have?
2. What are some ways people show their feelings?

2 What Can Help When You Feel Scared?

Did You Know?
Sometimes scared feelings can help people. Suppose someone is dared to do something dangerous. The person is scared to take the dare and decides not to do the dangerous thing. Scared feelings helped keep the person safe.

Jenny and some friends planned a play. Jenny is to play the part of a space traveler. She feels scared on the day of the play. Jenny wants to be in the play. At the same time, she does not want to be in the play. What can help Jenny's scared feelings?

Everyone feels scared at certain times. Remembering this might help you feel better when you are scared. You might have scared feelings when you start to learn new things. You might have scared feelings because you are afraid of not doing something well.

Sometimes talking about scared feelings helps you feel better. Talking with a family member, a friend, or a teacher might help you feel less scared.

Many times it helps to do what you feel scared about doing. Then your scared feelings might soon go away. You might not think about being scared if you are doing something. What is Jenny doing to help herself feel less scared?

Can you think of times when people might feel scared? What could help make their scared feelings go away?

Think Back • *Study on your own with Study Guide page 222.*

1. When might a person feel scared?
2. What might help when a person has scared feelings?

3 What Can Help When Feelings Are Hurt?

Glen laughed when Melissa made a mistake. Glen did not mean to hurt Melissa's feelings, but he did. Now Glen is feeling sad and worried. He knows he did an unkind thing. He thinks Melissa might not play with him anymore. What can Glen do to make things better?

You might want to talk to a family member if you have hurt someone's feelings. You might also talk to a friend. Ask for advice about how you can make the person whose feelings you hurt feel better.

Saying "I'm sorry" can help change hurt feelings.

Often saying two words can help change hurt feelings. The words are "I'm sorry." In the picture, Glen is saying these words to his friend Melissa. How can saying "I'm sorry" help?

Suppose a person often says or does unkind things to others. Then, saying the words "I'm sorry" might not help change hurt feelings. The person must act differently so that he or she does not hurt the feelings of others.

On Your Own
The boy in the picture is saying "I'm sorry" to his friend. List on paper three other things he can do to help change his friend's hurt feelings.

Think Back • *Study on your own with Study Guide page 222.*

1. Who might give advice about how to make a person with hurt feelings feel better?
2. What two words can be said to help change hurt feelings?

4 What Can Help When a Pet Dies?

Danny had a dog named Sparky. Danny loved Sparky very much. Danny had his pet for six years. One day a car hit Sparky and the pet died. Danny felt very sad. What is Danny doing to help himself feel better?

Talking to family members might help a person whose pet has died. Family members often know that the person feels very sad. Family members might suggest ways to help the person feel better.

You might like to know how Danny's family helped him. What did different family members say to Danny?

Danny's grandfather said, "You go ahead and cry. Crying often helps a sad person feel better."

Danny's mother said, "You can always remember Sparky. Think of what you and Sparky liked to do together."

Danny's younger sister said, "I will draw a picture of Sparky for you. Then you can remember how Sparky looked."

What are some other ways family members might help a sad person feel better?

Talking to family members can help when a person feels sad.

Think Back • *Study on your own with Study Guide page 223.*

1. How might talking to family members help a person whose pet has died?
2. What can a person whose pet has died do to feel better?

Did You Know?
Smiling can often help change sad feelings to happy ones. If you feel sad sometimes, you might try thinking of something that would make you smile. See whether your sad feelings change.

5 What Can Help When Things Go Wrong?

Suppose you have a day when things go wrong. You are late for school. You lose your spelling paper. Two friends go off to play without you after school. How might you feel?

You might feel angry and upset when things go wrong. What could you do to help change these feelings?

You might try doing something active. Exercising can often help you feel better. You might go outdoors to play. You might toss a ball or run for a while.

You might do something you think you will enjoy. Doing something enjoyable can help you feel better when you feel angry and upset. What are these children enjoying doing?

You might do something for others to help yourself feel better. Maybe you can help at home in some way. Ask an adult in your family what you can do to help. You often feel better when you are busy. You might start to feel less angry and upset.

Think Back • *Study on your own with Study Guide page 223.*

1. How might a person feel when things go wrong?
2. What can a person do to help change angry and upset feelings?

Doing something enjoyable can sometimes help a person feel better.

Health Activities Workshop

Learning More About Feelings

1. Look at the puzzle. Read from left to right. Find the names of seven feelings all people have. Write the names on your own paper.

Z V N M S A D X X O P W
H A P P Y V X A N G R Y
Y R E S C A R E D X V C
O H U R T E W Q Q A Z X
E E P R O U D C C B N Y
V E T W W O R R I E D O

2. Make up a play about how family members can help a person whose pet has died. Ask your classmates to play the parts of family members.

3. This boy is drawing an activity that he enjoys doing. What activities do you enjoy doing? Draw yourself doing them. Keep your drawings. Look at them when you are feeling angry and upset. Choose one of the activities to do to help you feel better.

Looking at Careers

4. Do you like to draw pictures? You might want to be an **artist** if you do. Some artists go to a special art school. They learn to do different kinds of art, including drawing and painting.

Artists show their feelings through their work. People who look at works of art can have different feelings about them.

Some artists sell their artwork. Some artists teach art classes. Some artists draw pictures for books. Artists might also work for companies. The artists help make up advertisements for the companies. The advertisements are put on television or in newspapers and magazines.

Look at this painting. What feelings do you think the artist is trying to show? What feelings might a person have when looking at the painting?

You might like to find a book of paintings in a library. Think of the different feelings the paintings show.

sharing, using something together.

cooperation (kō op′ə rā′shən), working together with other people.

6 What Can Help You Get Along with Others?

Amy is feeling troubled and a little puzzled too. She has just had an argument with her younger brother. Each one wanted to use the same tube of glue. Amy and her brother argued about who would use the glue first. Amy sometimes asks herself, "Do all sisters and brothers have arguments?" How would you answer Amy's question?

People who love each other, such as people in a family, might argue at times. All sisters and brothers argue a little. However, too much arguing can upset people.

Why might sisters and brothers argue? Often they argue about taking turns or **sharing** games and toys. Sharing means using things together or dividing things up and each getting a part.

People in families can argue less if they learn to share. Sharing can also help you get along with others. How are Amy and her brother sharing here?

You also get along better with others if you work together to get jobs done. You show **cooperation** when you do your best to work with other people. Family members might show cooperation when doing jobs around the house. How could you show cooperation in other ways at home?

Sharing helps people
get along better.

consideration (kən sid′ə rā′shən), thinking about another person's feelings.

On Your Own
Make a list of ways you can show consideration for a new person. Try to list at least three ways. Use the ways if a new person comes to your classroom.

How Can Showing Consideration Help?

These children are asking a new student at their school to play with them. They know that a new person often feels lonely. They want the newcomer to feel happy. They are showing **consideration** for the new person.

Suppose you see a new person at school. The new person looks sad and lonely. He or she cannot hear well. You could show consideration by asking the person to choose a game to play. The newcomer might choose a game in which hearing well is not important.

How Can Showing Understanding Help?

understanding, knowing what another person is feeling.

Showing **understanding** for someone who makes a mistake can help the person feel better. You show understanding when you try to think of how another person feels. You might say this to a person who makes a mistake: "Try not to feel bad. You're not the only one who ever makes mistakes."

Think Back • *Study on your own with Study Guide page 223.*

1. How can sharing help people?
2. How can showing consideration for a new person help him or her?
3. How can you show understanding when someone makes a mistake?

Vikki Carr Sings Away Her Shyness

Vikki Carr is a famous singer who sings in concerts and on television. She has even sung at the White House for two United States Presidents. She sings in English and in Spanish. Many people enjoy listening to her.

Vikki Carr has always enjoyed singing. However, as a young girl she was shy. Her teachers did not think she would go into show business because of her shyness. Vikki Carr had to get over her shy feelings to be a singer. She went on stage even though she felt shy. She got over being shy after singing in front of people many times.

Look at the picture of Vikki Carr singing. What do you think she is feeling? How would you feel if you were singing in front of many people? Vikki Carr is proud to sing on stage.

Talk About It

1. How did Vikki Carr get over her shy feelings?
2. What could feeling less shy help a person do?

Vikki Carr singing the National Anthem at a political convention

Chapter 1 Review

Reviewing Lesson Objectives

1. Tell ways people can show feelings. (pages 18–19)
2. Tell what can help when a person has scared feelings. (pages 20–21)
3. Tell what two words can be said to help change hurt feelings. (pages 22–23)
4. Tell what a person whose pet has died can do to feel better. (pages 24–25)
5. Tell what a person can do to help change angry and upset feelings. (pages 26–27)
6. Tell how sharing and showing cooperation, consideration, and understanding help a person. (pages 30–33)

For further review, use Study Guide pages 222-223.

Checking Health Vocabulary

Number your paper from 1–5. Match each meaning in Column I with the correct word in Column II.

Column I	*Column II*
1. the way a person feels about something	a. consideration
2. using something together	b. cooperation
3. working together with other people	c. feelings
4. thinking about another person's feelings	d. sharing
5. knowing what another person is feeling	e. understanding

Number your paper from 6–9. Next to each number write the word that best completes each sentence in the paragraph. Choose the words from the list below.

enjoys   exercising   others   upset

A person might feel __(6)__ when things go wrong. Sometimes __(7)__ can help the person feel better. Doing something he or she __(8)__ can help too. Often doing something for __(9)__ helps a person feel better.

Chapter 1 Test

Complete the Sentence

Number your paper from 1–8. Next to each number write the word that best completes the sentence. Choose the words from the list below.

faces	scared
family	share
hurt	stand
others	understanding

1. Sometimes people's ____ show their feelings.
2. Sometimes people show feelings in the way they ____ or move.
3. Many times ____ feelings go away if a person goes ahead and does something.
4. Often saying "I'm sorry" can change ____ feelings.
5. Talking to ____ members might help a person whose pet has died.
6. Doing something for ____ might help a person feel less angry and upset.
7. People in families might argue less if they learn to ____.
8. Showing ____ for someone who makes a mistake can help the person feel better.

Short Answer

Number your paper from 9–15. Next to each number write the word or words that best answer the question.

9. What are happiness, anger, disappointment, and surprise?
10. What might a scared person remember to feel less scared?
11. What should a person do if he or she often hurts others' feelings?
12. How might crying help a sad person?
13. What is an activity that a person might do to feel less angry or upset?
14. How might family members show cooperation at home?
15. What might people show for a newcomer to help them feel happy?

Essay

Write the answers on your paper. Use complete sentences.

16. What are some ways you might show cooperation at school?
17. What are some ways you might show understanding for your classmates?

Health at Home

Having Happy Feelings

Do you like it when people at home have happy feelings? You can make even more of those happy feelings. You might do this activity.

Each week, find something kind or helpful to do for people in your family. Do not tell what you will do. Just go ahead and be kind or helpful. Then wait to see what happens.

What is this girl doing? How might she make a person feel happy? What could you do at home to be kind or helpful?

Reading at Home

Beginning to Learn About Feelings by Richard L. Allington and Kathleen Cowles. Raintree, 1980. Read about the different feelings that people have.

Team Work by George Ancona. T. Y. Crowell, 1983. Discover how people depend on each other to get a job done.

Chapter 2

Food and Your Health

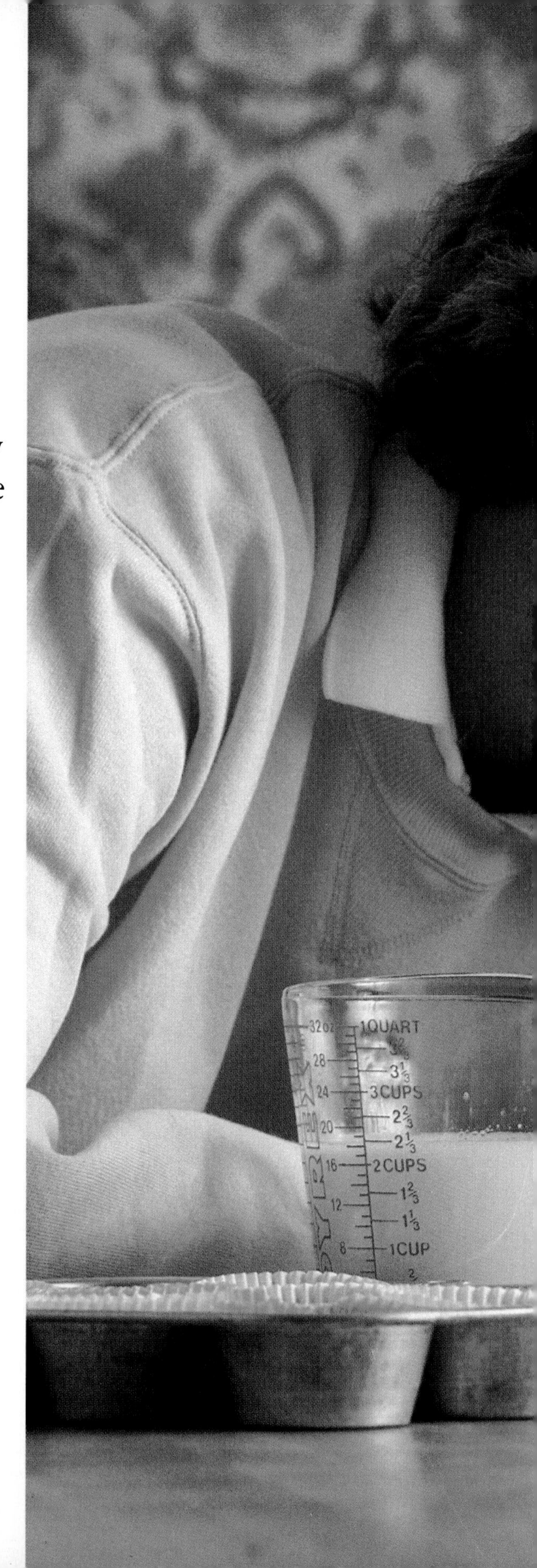

What makes this snack healthy? Only healthy foods are being used to make these bran muffins. What foods would you choose to make a healthy snack?

The lessons in this chapter will help you make healthy food choices. You will learn healthy ways to prepare food. Knowing how to choose, prepare, and serve healthy food can help keep you healthy throughout your life.

1 What Can Help You Make Healthy Food Choices?
2 What Are Some Healthy Meals?
3 What Different Vegetables Can You Eat?
4 How Can You Make Healthy Snack Choices?
5 How Can You Be a Wise Food Shopper?
6 What Are Healthy Ways to Prepare and Serve Food?

nutrient (nü′trē ənt), a substance from food that is needed for health and growth.

1 What Can Help You Make Healthy Food Choices?

A grocery store has many different kinds of foods to choose from. Most of the foods are in attractive packages. People often have a difficult time deciding which foods to buy. Think of the reasons why you choose the foods you do. You might choose foods because you like their taste, smell, or color.

Eric and his mother are shopping for groceries. How can Eric's mother decide which foods her family needs?

Eric's mother uses the four food group plan to help her choose healthy foods. Your family and you can use this plan too. The plan tells what four main kinds of foods you need every day. The plan also tells how much of each kind of food to eat.

Eric and his mother are using the four food group plan to make healthy food choices.

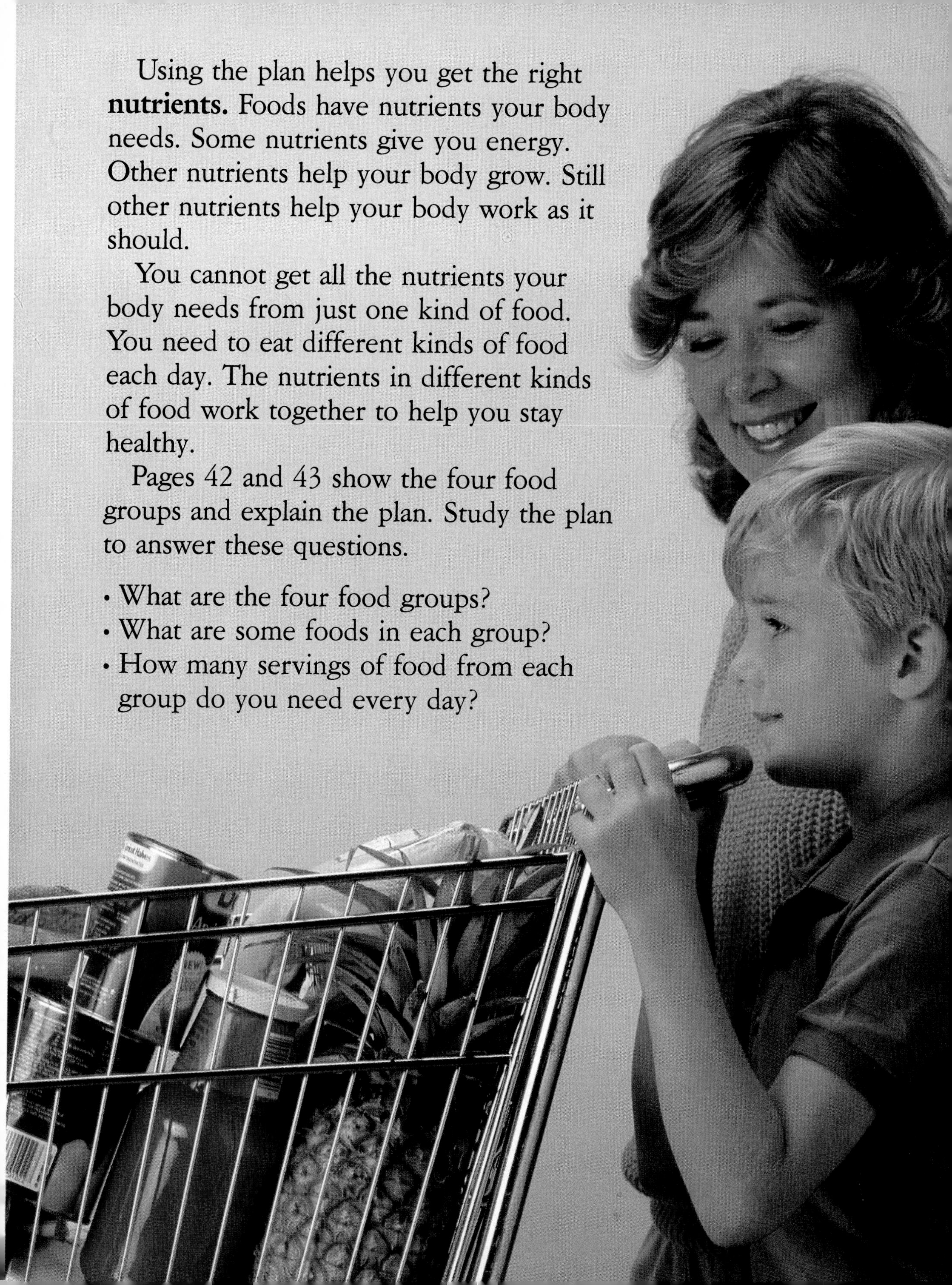

Using the plan helps you get the right **nutrients.** Foods have nutrients your body needs. Some nutrients give you energy. Other nutrients help your body grow. Still other nutrients help your body work as it should.

You cannot get all the nutrients your body needs from just one kind of food. You need to eat different kinds of food each day. The nutrients in different kinds of food work together to help you stay healthy.

Pages 42 and 43 show the four food groups and explain the plan. Study the plan to answer these questions.

- What are the four food groups?
- What are some foods in each group?
- How many servings of food from each group do you need every day?

vegetable-fruit group, the food group that has vegetables and fruits.

bread-cereal group, the food group that has grains and foods made from grains.

What Are the Four Food Groups?

The pictures show the four food groups. Find out how each group can help your body. One food group has grains and foods made from grains. What is the name of this group? What foods are in the same group as meat?

Vegetable-fruit group

Most of the nutrients in these foods help your body work as it should. You need four servings from the **vegetable-fruit group** each day.

Bread-cereal group

Most of the nutrients in these foods give your body energy. You need four servings from the **bread-cereal group** each day.

Think Back • *Study on your own with Study Guide page 224.*

1. What can be used to help make healthy food choices?
2. How do nutrients help keep the body healthy?
3. What are the names of the four food groups?
4. How many servings from each food group are needed each day?

meat-poultry-fish-bean group, the food group that has meats, poultry, fish, nuts, eggs, and beans.

milk-cheese group, the food group that has milk and foods made from milk.

Meat-poultry-fish-bean group

Most of the nutrients in these foods help your body grow. You need two servings from the **meat-poultry-fish-bean group** each day.

Milk-cheese group

The foods in this group have many different kinds of nutrients. Some nutrients help your body grow. Some nutrients give you energy. Some help your body work as it should. You need three servings from the **milk-cheese group** each day.

2 What Are Some Healthy Meals?

Look at what Jill ate one day for breakfast, lunch, and supper. Did she eat healthy meals?

Jill ate foods from each of the four food groups. Healthy meals for a day have foods from each food group. Jill had orange juice, vegetable soup, an apple, and salad from the vegetable-fruit group. She had oatmeal, toast, rice, and a roll from the bread-cereal group. She had peanut butter and chicken from the meat group. From the milk-cheese group she had yogurt and two glasses of milk.

Healthy meals for a day

Healthy meals for a day have enough servings from each food group. Jill had enough servings from each group. She ate four servings from the vegetable-fruit group. She ate four servings from the bread-cereal group. She ate two servings from the meat group and three servings from the milk-cheese group.

Suppose you were planning Jill's meals for tomorrow. What foods would your menu have to give Jill energy? What foods on the menu would help her body grow? What foods would help Jill's body work as it should?

How Can You Decide If a Day's Meals Are Healthy?

Be a food detective. Look at the meals Mike ate one day. Decide if Mike had healthy meals. Use the four food group plan to help you decide.

First, find out if Mike had foods from each of the four food groups. Look back at pages 42 and 43 if you need help.

Now, find out if Mike had enough servings from each food group. Make a chart like this one to help you decide.

What did you find out about Mike's meals?

	Breakfast	Lunch	Supper	Total servings
Vegetable-fruit group 4 servings				4
Bread-cereal group 4 servings				
Meat-poultry-fish-bean group 2 servings				
Milk-cheese group 3 servings				

Think Back • *Study on your own with Study Guide page 224.*

1. How can the four food group plan be used to have healthy meals for a day?
2. What are some foods that can make up a healthy breakfast?
3. What are some foods that can make up a healthy lunch?
4. What are some foods that can make up a healthy supper?

3 What Different Vegetables Can You Eat?

Eat these kinds of vegetables three or four times weekly.

You have been doing some detective work. You checked Mike's meals and found that he was eating healthy meals.

Some other children did some detective work too. They studied what vegetables they were eating. They found out they were eating many different vegetables.

You need to eat different kinds of vegetables. Different kinds of vegetables give you different kinds of nutrients. Your body needs these nutrients to stay healthy.

All of the vegetables you eat come from parts of plants. For example, you are eating the leaves of a plant when you eat spinach. A carrot is the root of a plant.

Try to eat leafy, green, or dark yellow vegetables three or four times a week. What green vegetables do you see in the picture? Which green vegetables are leafy? What dark yellow vegetables do you see?

Which vegetables do you like? Why do you like them? Do you like their colors? What special way do you like them served?

Look again at the vegetables. Which are fresh? What other ways can you see to buy vegetables?

On Your Own
Frank is eating lunch at a friend's home. Frank has never tasted the green vegetable that his friend is eating. Frank is trying to decide if he should eat the vegetable or not. What do you think Frank should do? Write a paragraph explaining why you think as you do.

Think Back • *Study on your own with Study Guide page 224.*

1. What kinds of vegetables should be eaten three or four times a week?
2. How can eating different kinds of vegetables help keep the body healthy?

Learning More About Healthy Foods

1. Look at the sandwich. It has foods in it from each of the four food groups. What are the foods?

Think of a sandwich you could make. List the different kinds of food in your sandwich. Try to have a food from each food group in it.

2. Guess the answer to this riddle.

This food is in the vegetable-fruit group.
You can eat it raw or cooked.
It is a red color.
Its name starts with T.
What is it?

3. Think of a vegetable you like. Write a few sentences about it. Tell why you like the vegetable. Get an idea from what one boy wrote about why he likes corn.

You might draw a picture to go with your story.

Why I Like Corn

I like the color of corn. I like the smell of corn cooking. I like the crunch, crunch when I chew corn.

Looking at Careers

4. A **dietitian** plans meals for schools, hospitals, nursing homes, and some restaurants. He or she tries to make the meals as healthy as possible. A dietitian might also teach people how to plan more healthy meals. Would you enjoy this job? You need to go to college for four years to be a dietitian.

Maybe you know a dietitian. Ask the person to tell you about his or her work. You also might look for a book that tells what a dietitian does. Ask a librarian to help you.

4 How Can You Make Healthy Snack Choices?

Joe will celebrate his birthday at school. His mother is bringing some healthy snacks to school. The snacks are not too sweet or salty.

Sweet snacks, such as cake and candy, are not very healthy. These snacks can stick to your teeth and harm them. Try not to choose too many sweet, sticky snacks.

Suppose you are thirsty between meals. Choose a healthy drink. Try fruit juices, milk, or water.

Try not to eat too many salty snacks. Healthy snacks have little salt added to them. Many foods from the four food groups have salt in them. You get enough salt from these foods in your meals. You do not need to add more.

Choosing healthy snacks can help you get food you need each day. Suppose you do not get enough servings of fruits and vegetables in your meals. What snacks could you choose to make up the servings?

Joe is getting ready to serve some healthy snacks at his birthday party.

On Your Own
Make a list of the healthy snacks you see in the picture. Then think of five more healthy snacks and add them to the list.

What Are Some Healthy Snacks?

You can see the healthy snacks Joe's mother brought to school. What food groups are they from?

You could make some changes and still have healthy snacks. You might have green pepper slices instead of celery. What other fruit drinks might you have?.

Think Back • *Study on your own with Study Guide 225.*

1. What should a person think about when choosing healthy snacks?
2. How can eating healthy snacks help you get food you need each day?
3. What are some healthy snacks from the four food groups?

Healthy snacks

Learning More About Healthy Snacks

1. Look at the different ways to serve peanut butter. Draw pictures of some different ways to serve eggs, carrots, tomatoes, or potatoes. The pictures show some ways to serve these foods.

2. Go to a library and find a cookbook for children. Use the cookbook to help you plan a healthy snack. Ask a parent for permission to make the snack at home.

5 How Can You Be a Wise Food Shopper?

Maria's father asked her to buy a can of fruit juice for breakfast. He said, "Buy a large can of fruit juice. Be sure you get real fruit juice." Maria wants to be a wise food shopper. What should she do?

Maria should read the labels on the cans. The labels can tell Maria what she needs to know. For example, a label can tell if a can has all real fruit juice in it. Some drinks have only flavor, water, and sugar in them. Notice the labels on the cans. Which can has all real fruit juice in it?

Maria should also look at the prices of the cans. Then she can find out which kind of fruit juice will cost the least.

The label tells what is inside a can.

Maria should be willing to try different kinds of foods. For example, she could try the kind of fruit juice that costs the least. The best tasting foods do not always cost the most. You can often find good tasting foods at lower prices. How do you find out if these foods taste good? Be willing to try them.

Suppose the kind of food that costs the least does not taste good. The wise food shopper will not buy that kind again.

Did You Know?
Some cities have markets where farmers can sell their crops. The fruits and vegetables are sometimes fresher and cheaper than those in a supermarket.

Think Back • *Study on your own with Study Guide page 225.*

1. What can a wise food shopper learn from reading labels?
2. What can a wise food shopper learn from looking at prices?
3. What can a wise food shopper learn from trying different kinds of foods?

Learning More About Food Choices

1. Make up a play. Pretend you are in a food store with a friend. The friend wants to buy a can of baked beans. What can you tell your friend about making wise food choices?

2. Write a short story about choosing a new food for your family. Be sure to tell what the food is. You might also write why you would choose it. Do you think your story shows you made a wise food choice? Explain your answer.

3. Sometimes stores have food sales. Some foods will cost less than usual. The stores have signs like these that tell about their food sales. Make up a sign for a food sale. Tell how your sign could help a food shopper.

6 What Are Healthy Ways to Prepare and Serve Food?

Suppose you are going to help make supper. What should you do first?

You should wash your hands with soap and warm water. You will wash away germs that can cause disease. Germs will not get on foods you touch if your hands are clean.

Wash any fresh fruits and vegetables too. You will wash away harmful germs and chemicals when you wash them. You will also wash off dirt.

Be sure you use clean pans, dishes, and spoons. Wash the tabletop you work on as well. Why should you do this?

When you finish eating, put some leftover foods in the refrigerator. Germs can grow in certain foods that get warm. Germs do not grow as quickly in cold places. The picture shows foods that should be kept in a refrigerator. What leftover foods do you see?

Think Back • *Study on your own with Study Guide page 225.*

1. How can washing hands before preparing food help prevent disease?
2. How does washing fresh fruits and vegetables help keep a person healthy?
3. What is a healthy way to store leftover foods?

These foods should be kept in a refrigerator.

Making Milk Safe to Drink

Is milk one of your favorite drinks? Then you might want to say thank you to Louis Pasteur. He helped make milk safe for you to drink.

Louis Pasteur was born in France in 1822. As a child, he was interested in learning about science. Pasteur became a science teacher when he grew up.

One of Louis Pasteur's special interests was studying germs. He learned that germs in the air could get into food. He also learned that some germs in food can cause disease.

Louis Pasteur noticed that some people got sick after they drank milk. Some of these people died. Pasteur wanted to make milk safe for people to drink. He worked until he found a way to kill the harmful germs in milk.

Pasteur discovered that heating milk to a certain temperature kills harmful germs. Then the milk is safe to drink. This way of making milk safe to drink is named for Louis Pasteur. It is known as pasteurization. Most dairies now pasteurize milk.

Talk About It

1. How did Louis Pasteur help make milk safe to drink?
2. What are some other foods that are safe to eat because of Louis Pasteur's discovery?

Chapter 2 Review

Reviewing Lesson Objectives

1. Tell the number of daily servings needed from each food group. (pages 40–43)
2. Tell how using the food group plan helps in planning healthy meals for a day. (pages 44–47)
3. Tell what kinds of vegetables should be eaten three or four times a week. (pages 48–49)
4. Tell what to think about when choosing healthy snacks and list some healthy snacks. (pages 52–54)
5. Tell how to be a wise food shopper. (pages 56–57)
6. Tell healthy ways to prepare, serve, and keep foods. (pages 60–61)

For further review, use Study Guide pages 224–225.

Checking Health Vocabulary

Number your paper from 1–5. Match each meaning in Column I with the correct word or words in Column II.

Column I

1. a substance from food needed for health and growth
2. the food group with foods made from grain
3. the food group made up of vegetables and fruits
4. the food group that has meats, poultry, fish, nuts, eggs, and beans
5. the food group with milk and foods made from milk

Column II

a. bread-cereal group
b. meat-poultry-fish-bean group
c. milk-cheese group
d. nutrient
e. vegetable-fruit group

Chapter 2 Test

Complete the Sentence

Number your paper from 1–8. Next to each number write the word that best completes the sentence. Choose the words from the list below.

four	nutrients
germs	snacks
labels	three
meals	vegetables

1. Food has ___ the body needs.
2. The number of servings needed each day from the milk-cheese group is ___.
3. The number of servings needed each day from the vegetable-fruit group is ___.
4. Healthy ___ for a day have foods from four food groups.
5. Leafy, green, or dark yellow ___ should be eaten three or four times a week.
6. Eating fruits for ___ can help make up needed daily servings.
7. Reading ___ helps a wise food shopper find out what is in food.
8. Washing fresh fruits and vegetables removes harmful ___ and chemicals.

Short Answer

Number your paper from 9–15. Next to each number write the word or words that best answer the question.

9. How many daily servings are needed from the bread-cereal group?
10. How many daily servings are needed from the meat-poultry-fish-bean group?
11. What can be used to help plan healthy meals for the day?
12. What do vegetables contain to help keep the body healthy?
13. What kinds of snacks can harm the teeth?
14. What can a food shopper do to find out if a food tastes good?
15. Why are some leftover foods kept in a refrigerator?

Essay

Write the answers on your paper. Use complete sentences.

16. How does your favorite snack help you stay healthy?
17. How can trying new foods help you stay healthy?

Planning Healthy Snacks with Your Family

You have learned what healthy snacks are. What can you tell your family about such snacks?

You could make plans with your family for a snack spot in your refrigerator. The picture shows some snacks you might want to put in your snack spot. Family members might take turns preparing the snacks. Decide on times to eat the snacks.

Reading at Home

Night Markets: Bringing Food to a City by Joshua Horwitz. Crowell, 1984. Find out how food is brought to a large city each day to be sold.

What's On Your Plate? by Norah Smaridge. Abingdon, 1982. Find out how eating certain foods helps keep your body healthy.

Chapter 3

You and Your Body

What is this older sister helping her brother find out about himself? You can measure yourself each year to find out how much you have grown. What makes your body grow?

The lessons in this chapter will help you find out how your body grows and works. You might be able to take better care of your body if you understand how it works. Taking good care of your body can help keep you healthy now and in the future.

1 What Are You Made Of?
2 How Do Your Muscles and Bones Help You?
3 How Do Your Brain and Nerves Help You?
4 How Does Your Heart Help You?
5 How Do Your Lungs Help You?
6 How Do Your Stomach and Intestines Help You?
7 How Does Your Body Grow?

KAREN - AGE 9
KAREN - AGE 5
TODD - AGE 5
TODD - AGE 3
KAREN - AGE 3

cell (sel), the smallest living part of the body.

1 What Are You Made Of?

The outside of you is made up of skin, hair, and nails. Inside you are such things as bones, muscles, nerves, and blood.

Every part of you is made up of very tiny living parts. Each tiny part is a **cell.** You are made of millions of cells.

Your body is made of many different kinds of cells. Each kind is a different size and shape. Each kind does a different job.

You need a microscope to see body cells.

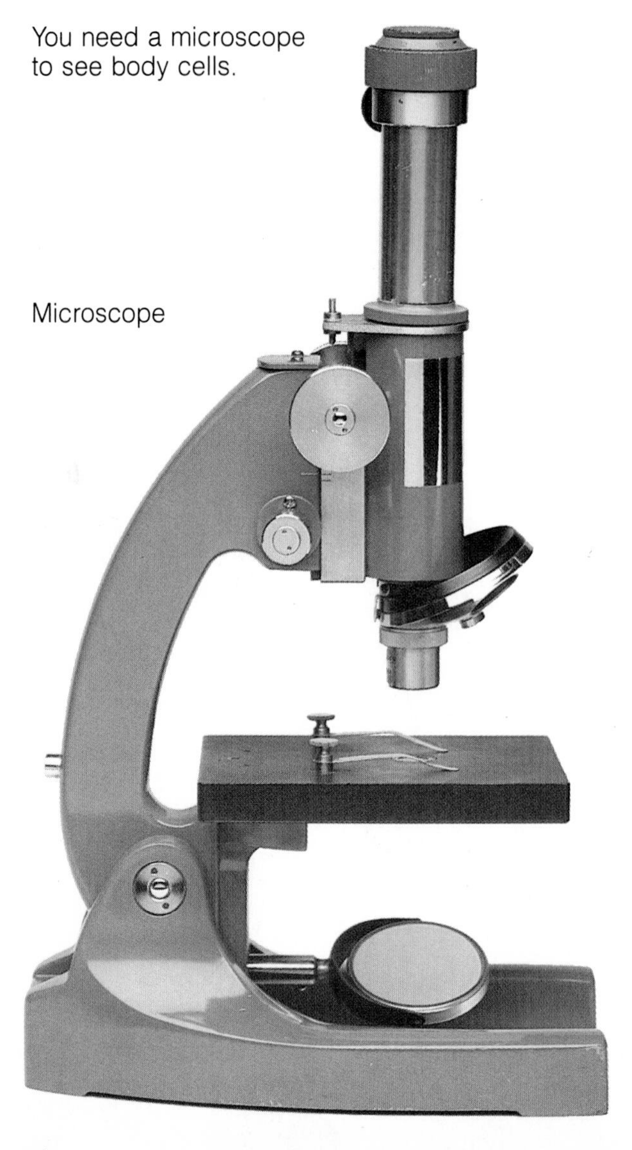

Microscope

Bone tissue

When many cells of the same kind are grouped together, they make up **tissue.** For example, many bone cells together make up bone tissue. Many muscle cells together make up muscle tissue. Many nerve cells together make up nerve tissue.

tissue (tish′ü), a group of cells that look alike.

Suppose you could look at different tissues through a microscope. You would see cells like these. Do the cells all look alike?

Think Back • *Study on your own with Study Guide page 226.*

1. What are the smallest living parts of the body?
2. What makes up tissue?
3. What is needed to see body cells?

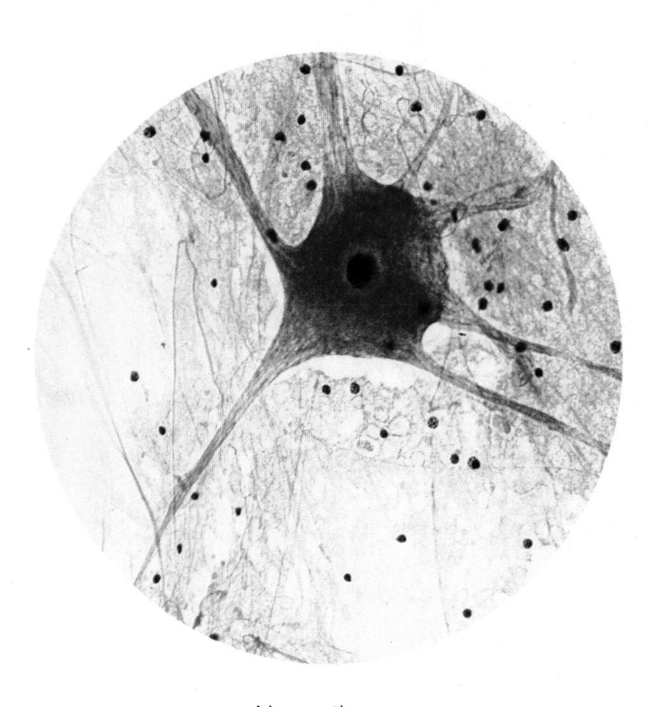

Nerve tissue

Muscle tissue

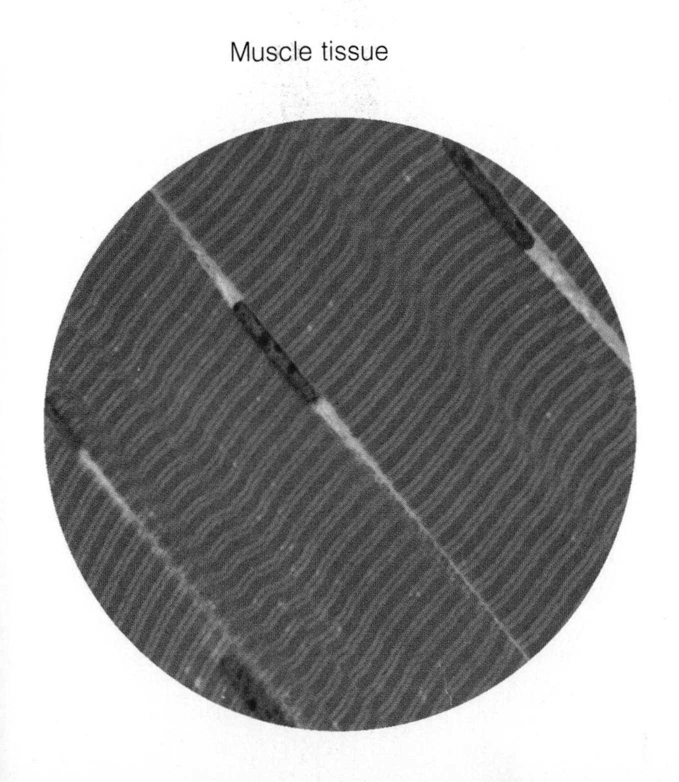

2 How Do Your Muscles and Bones Help You?

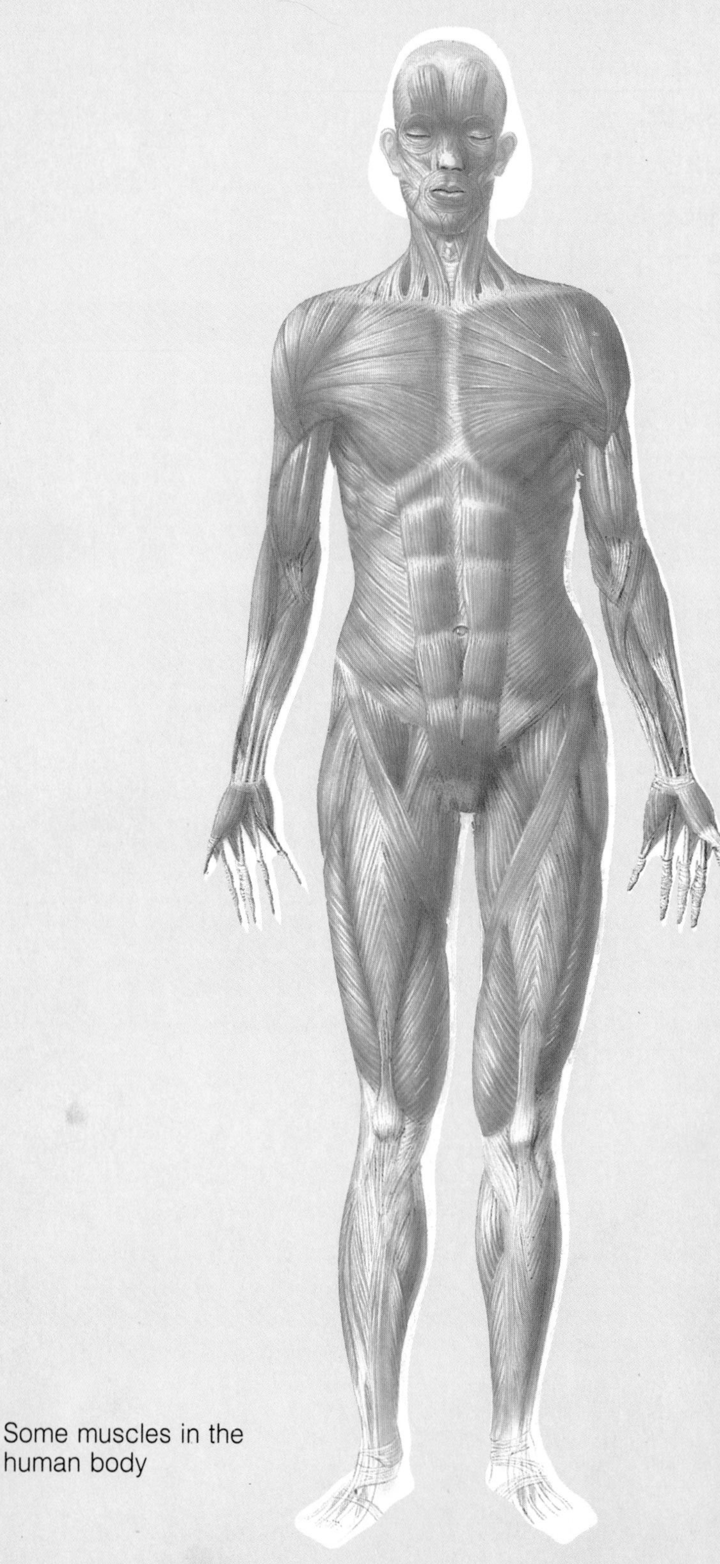

Some muscles in the human body

Look at the picture. It shows where muscles are in the body. Where can you find long muscles and short muscles? Where can you find flat ones?

Muscles give your body shape. Muscles also help you move about. Muscles are attached to your bones. The muscles pull the bones. The pulling makes the bones move.

Bend an arm. A muscle pulls your lower arm bones toward your upper arm bone. Straighten your arm. Another muscle pulls the lower arm bones away from the upper bone. The muscles in your body work in pairs to let you bend. Now feel the inside of your upper arm while you bend your arm.

Straighten your arm. Can you feel your muscles working to move your arm?

Your bones are under your muscles. You have more than two hundred bones in your body. All your bones together make up your skeleton.

Your bones help hold you up. Your bones and muscles help you move about. Your bones help give your body its shape. Some of your bones help protect parts of your body.

Notice the different kinds of bones in the skeleton. Some bones are long and some are short. Some bones are flat and some are round. Each bone has a special job to do.

Can you feel the bones in your head? What do they protect inside your head?

Did You Know?
The colored part of your eye is made of a muscle tissue. It makes the opening in the center of your eye smaller when you look at a bright light. Then the bright light will not harm your eye.

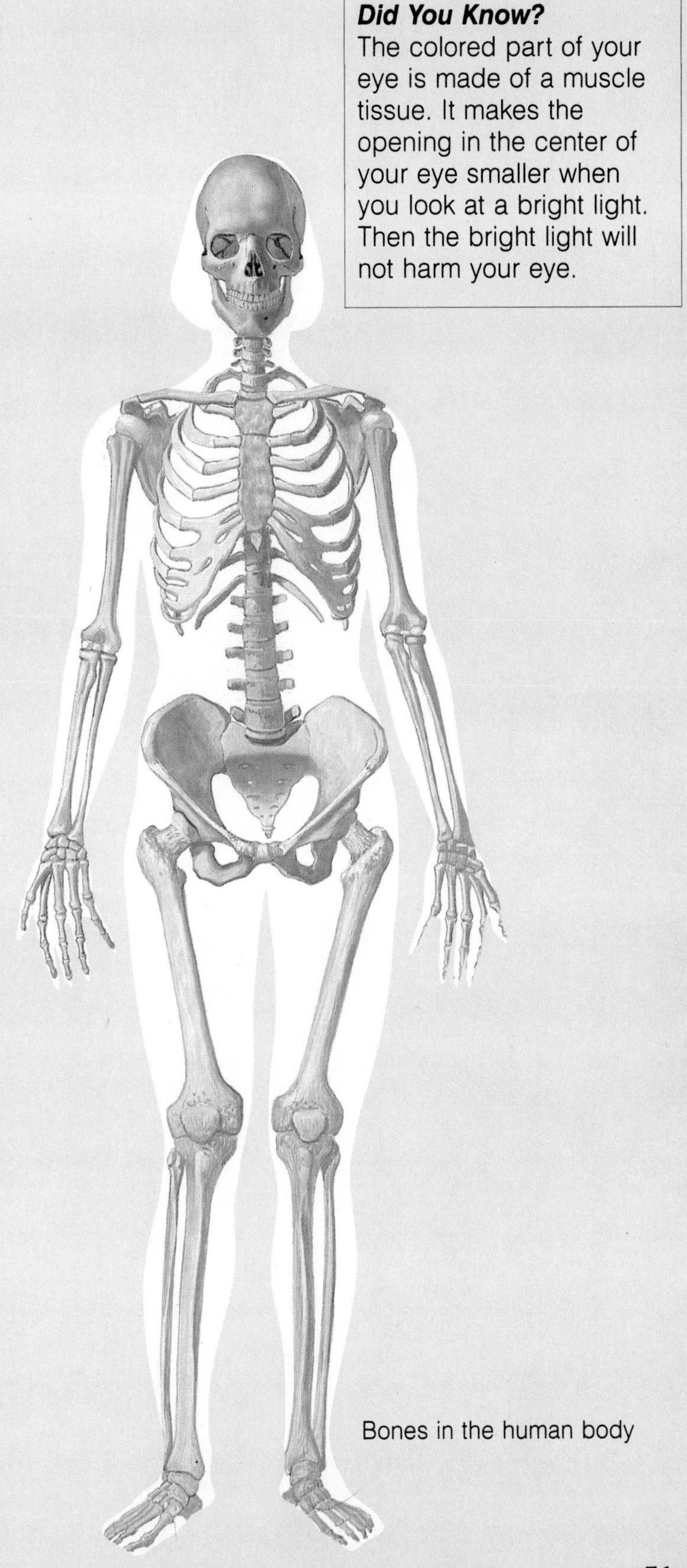

Bones in the human body

How Do Your Joints Help You?

Joints are the places in the skeleton where the bones fit together. Different joints let you move in different ways. The picture shows a joint in the body. You can kick a ball because of your knee joint. It lets you move your leg back and forth. Your shoulder joint lets you swing a bat. It lets you move your arm back and forth and around and around.

Think Back • *Study on your own with Study Guide page 226.*

1. How do muscles and bones work together to move the body?
2. How do bones help the body?
3. What are different ways joints let the body move?

Knee joint

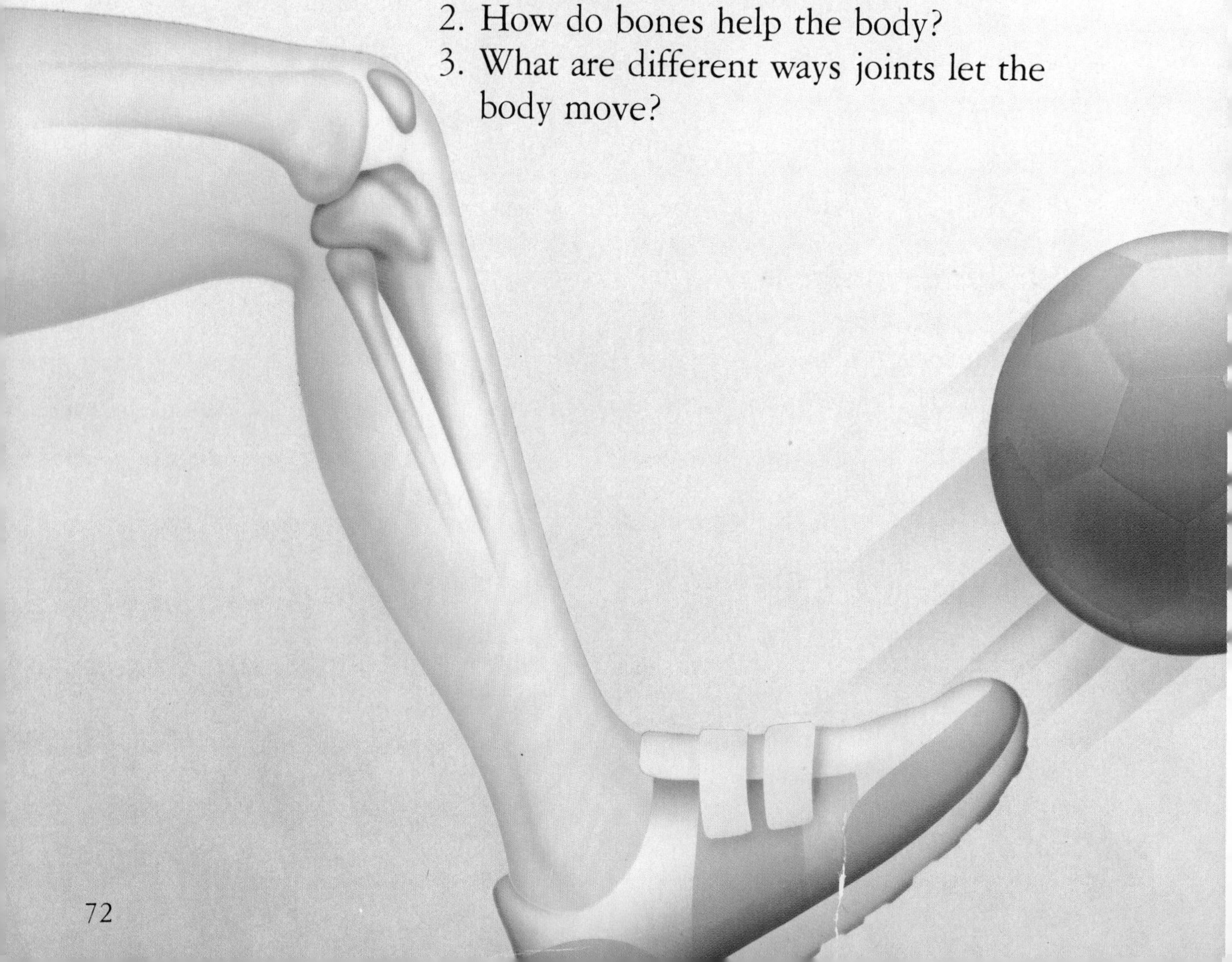

Using Muscles and Bones

1. The muscles in your face help you show your feelings. Think of the different feelings you show using muscles in your face. Move your face muscles to show these different feelings. See how many of your feelings other children can name.

2. You can find out which muscles help you move certain ways. Stand on your toes as shown for as long as possible. Feel which muscles are working. The muscle on the back of your lower leg pulls your heel up. This muscle helps you point your toe. Think of other actions you can do. Guess which muscles you would use when you perform these actions. Then try doing these actions and see if your guesses were correct.

3. Show how you would have to run if you had no knee joints. Then show how you would have to write if you had no elbow joint.

organ (ôr′gən), a group of different tissues that work together to do the same job.

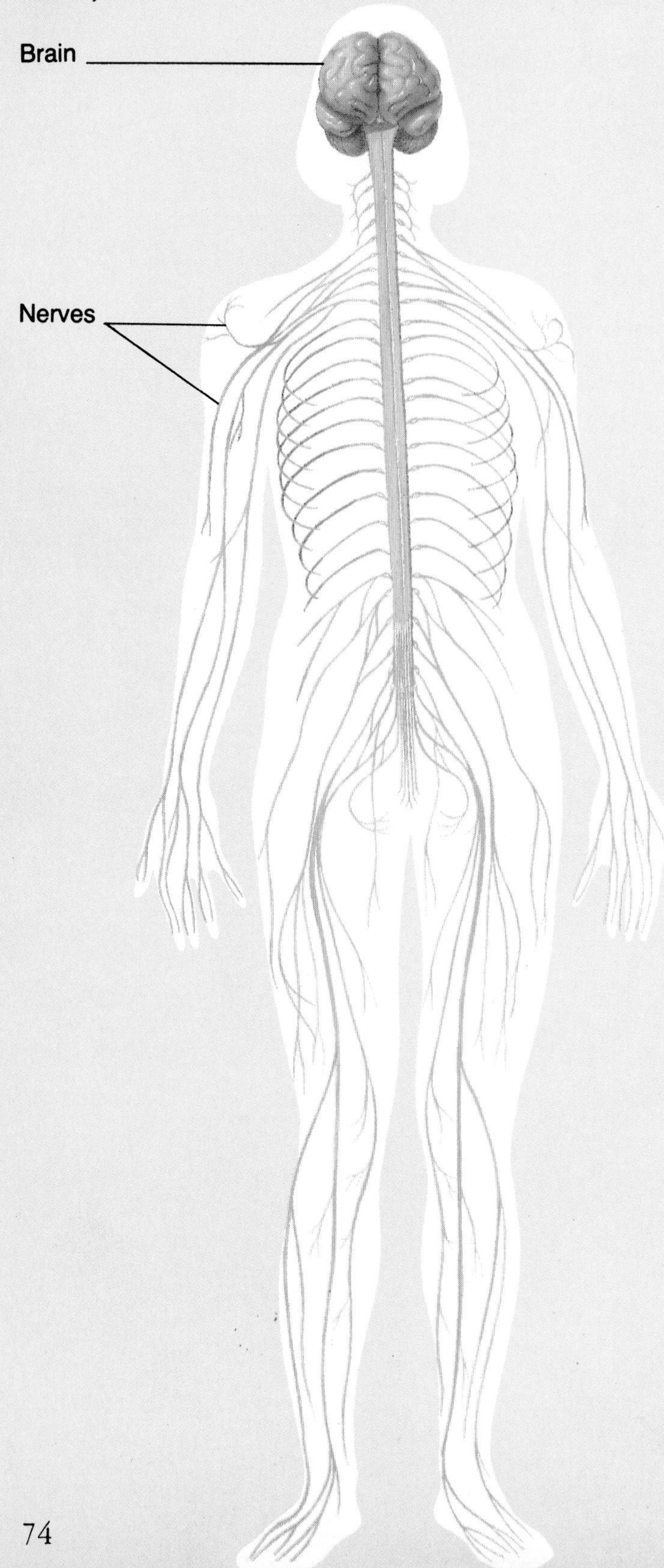

3 How Do Your Brain and Nerves Help You?

The brain is an **organ** inside your skull. It is made up of different kinds of tissues. The tissues all work together so you can think.

Messages go to your brain from all parts of your body. Your brain tells you what the messages mean. If you need to do something, your brain sends messages to your muscles. Your brain tells your muscles how to move.

Messages go to and from your brain over your nerves. Notice the nerves in the picture. Nerves are not all the same size. Some nerves are long and some are short. They go up and down the backbone. Nerves thread their way through most of the body.

What Do Your Senses Tell You?

You have five senses that send messages to your brain. The messages tell about seeing, hearing, touching, tasting, and smelling. For example, nerves in your eyes send messages about what you see to your brain. You do not really see until the messages get to your brain.

The picture shows the senses. What are they? What does each sense tell you?

Think Back • *Study on your own with Study Guide page 226.*

1. What is the job of the brain?
2. How do messages travel to and from the brain?
3. What are the five senses?

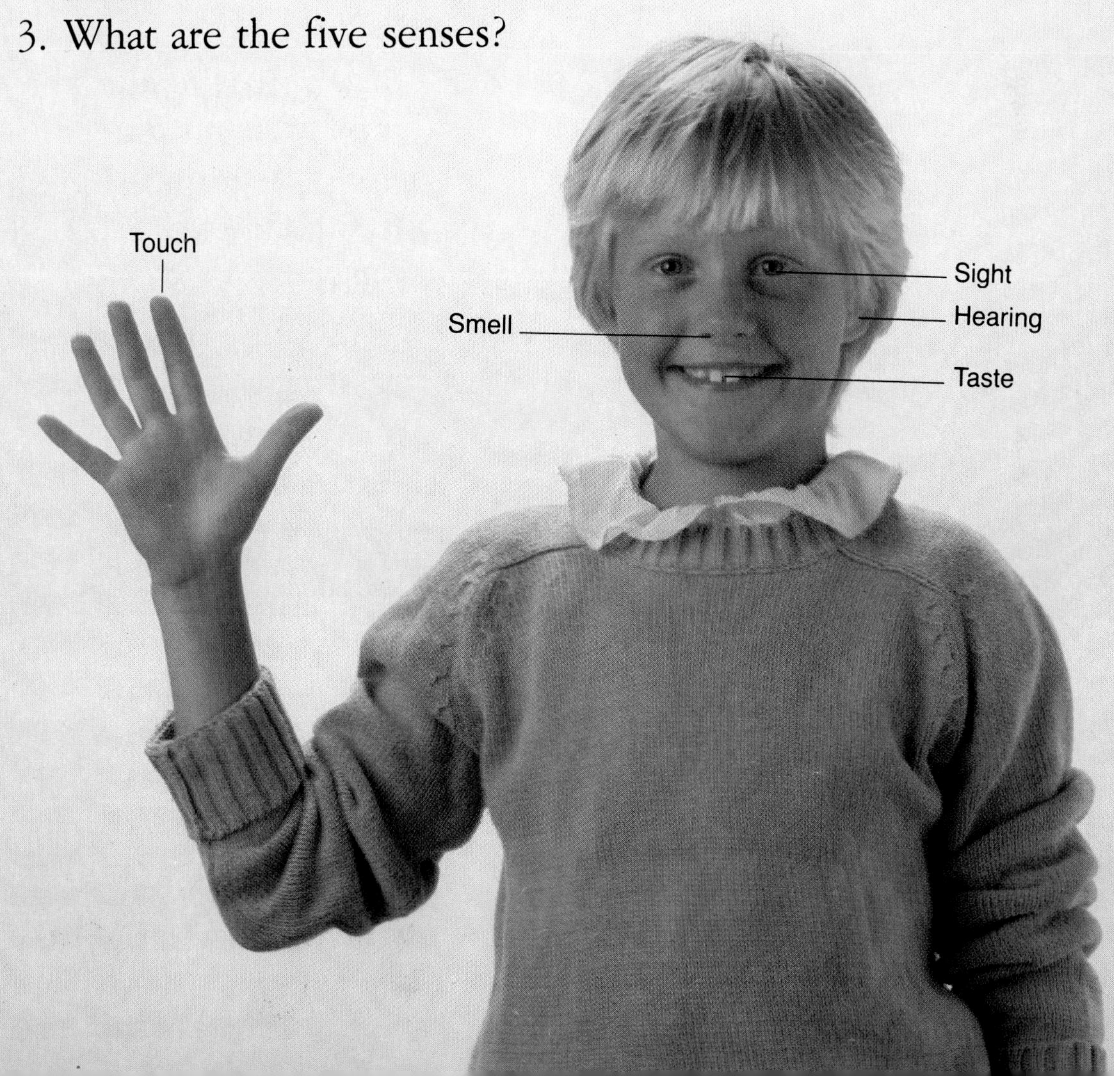

oxygen (ok′sə jən), a colorless gas cells take in to stay alive.

carbon dioxide (kär′bən dī ok′sīd), a colorless waste gas given off by the cells.

4 How Does Your Heart Help You?

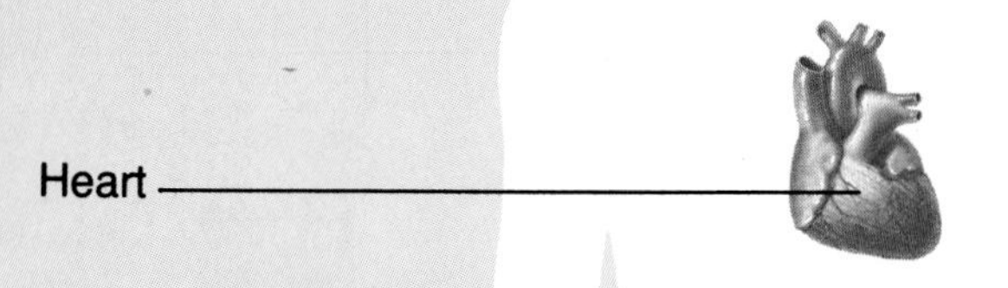

Look at the picture. Notice where the heart is in the chest. Now put your hand over your heart. Can you feel your heart beating?

Your heart beats all the time. It beats about 90 times a minute in a child your age.

Your heart is an organ. It is made mostly of muscle tissue. It pumps blood to all your cells. Blood carries **oxygen** to your cells. Oxygen is a gas that your cells need to stay alive. Blood also carries nutrients from food that your cells need.

Blood picks up a gas called **carbon dioxide** and other wastes from your cells. It carries the carbon dioxide and wastes away from your cells.

Your heart pumps blood into and through little tubes in your body. These tubes are your **blood vessels.** Find the blood vessels in the picture.

Your heart pumps blood to all parts of your body. The blood then travels through blood vessels back to your heart. The blood takes about one minute to travel from the heart and back.

blood vessel (ves′əl), a tube through which blood travels in the body.

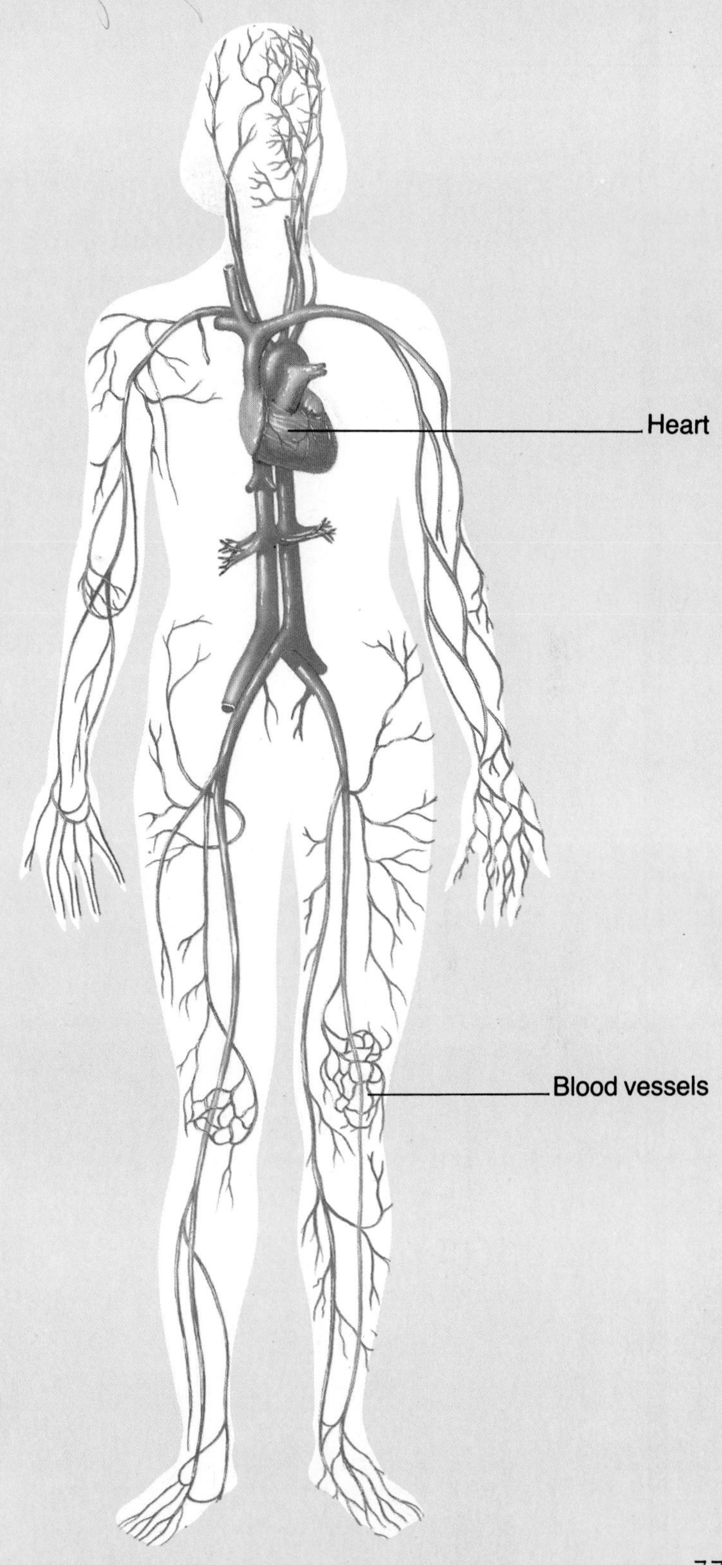

Think Back

- *See Study Guide on page 227.*

1. What is the job of the heart?
2. What does blood carry to the body's cells?
3. What does blood carry away from cells?
4. What does blood travel through in the body?

Did You Know?
Your lungs are light pink in color when you are a newborn baby. They become darker pink as you get older.

5 How Do Your Lungs Help You?

Your heart is in your chest. Your two lungs are also in your chest. The lungs are spongy organs that always have some air in them.

When you breathe in through your nose or mouth, air goes into your lungs. It goes down a long tube to get to your lungs.

Now try this. Put your hands on your chest as shown. Breathe in. What happens to your chest? Next breathe out. What happens to your chest?

Oxygen is in the air that you breathe into your lungs. You know your body cells must have oxygen to stay alive. How does oxygen get from your lungs to your cells?

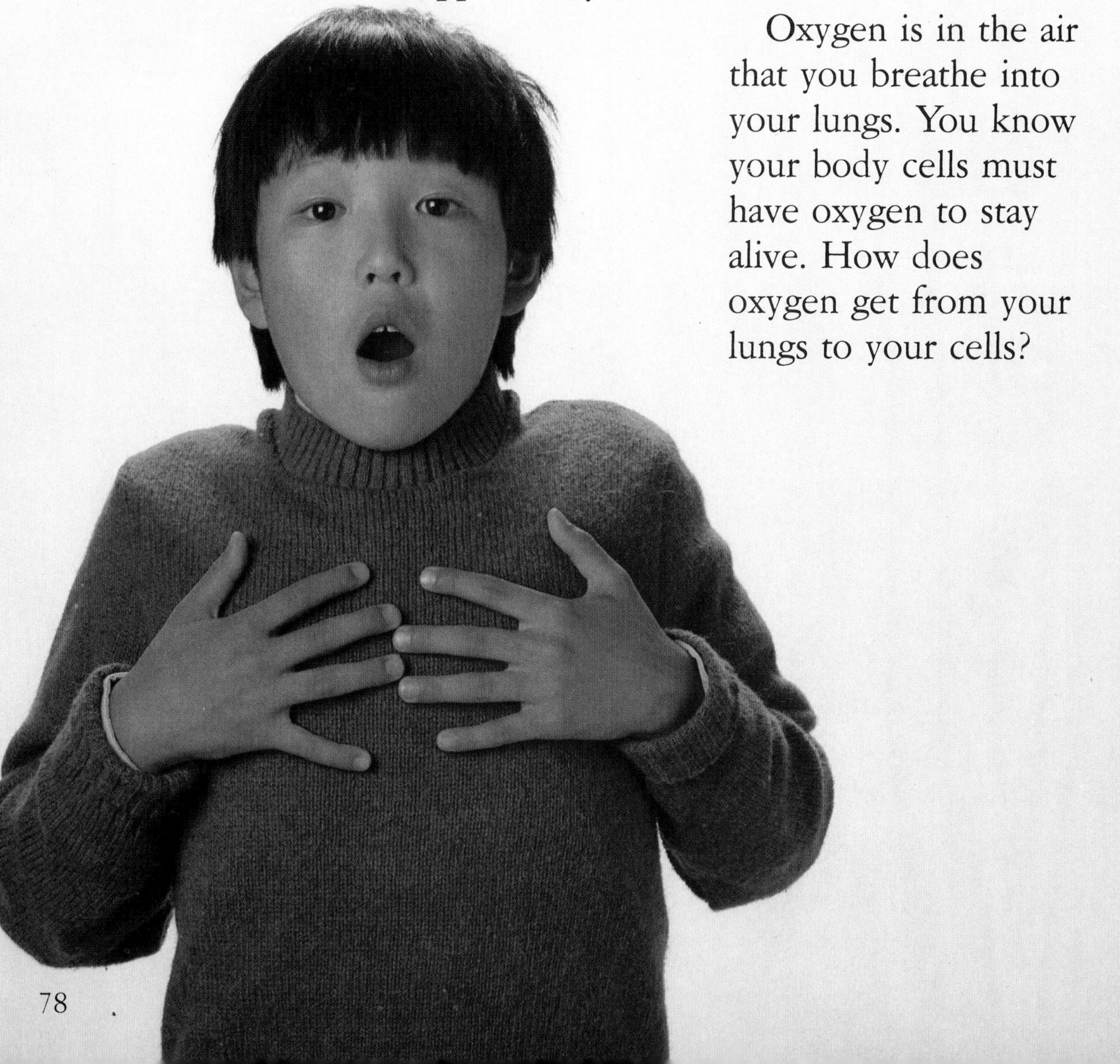

This boy can feel his chest get larger when he breathes.

Your heart pumps blood to your lungs through blood vessels. Find these vessels in the picture. The blood picks up oxygen in your lungs. Then the blood travels back to your heart. Next, your heart pumps out the blood to all of your cells. The blood leaves oxygen in your cells.

The blood picks up carbon dioxide in your cells. It carries the carbon dioxide to your heart. The blood with carbon dioxide then goes to your lungs. Your body gets rid of carbon dioxide when you breathe out.

On Your Own
You know that air goes into your lungs when you breathe. Write a paragraph telling why you think it is important for your lungs to breathe clean air.

Think Back

• *See Study Guide on page 227.*

1. How does oxygen get to the lungs?
2. How do body cells get the oxygen they need?
3. How does the body get rid of carbon dioxide?

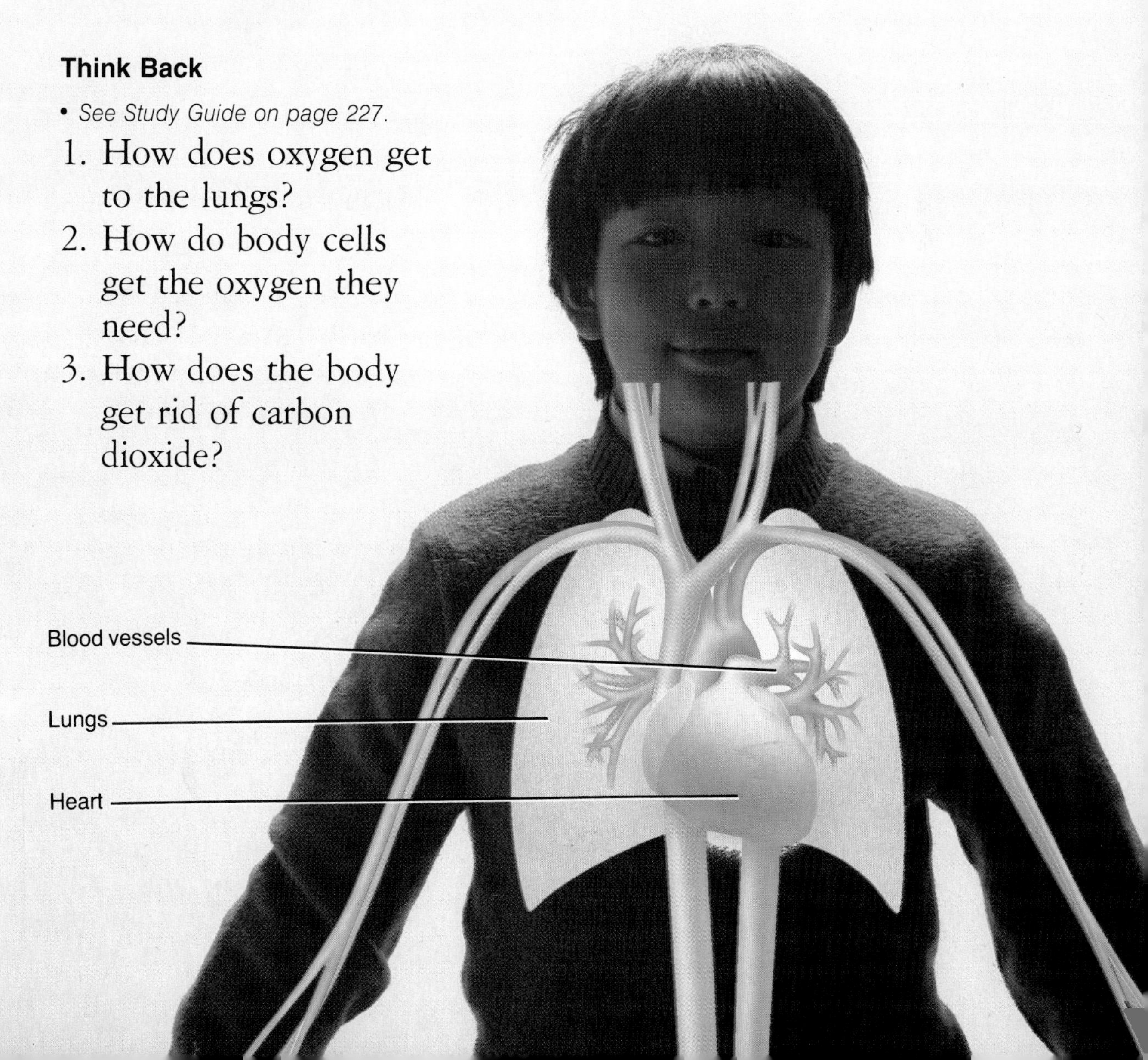

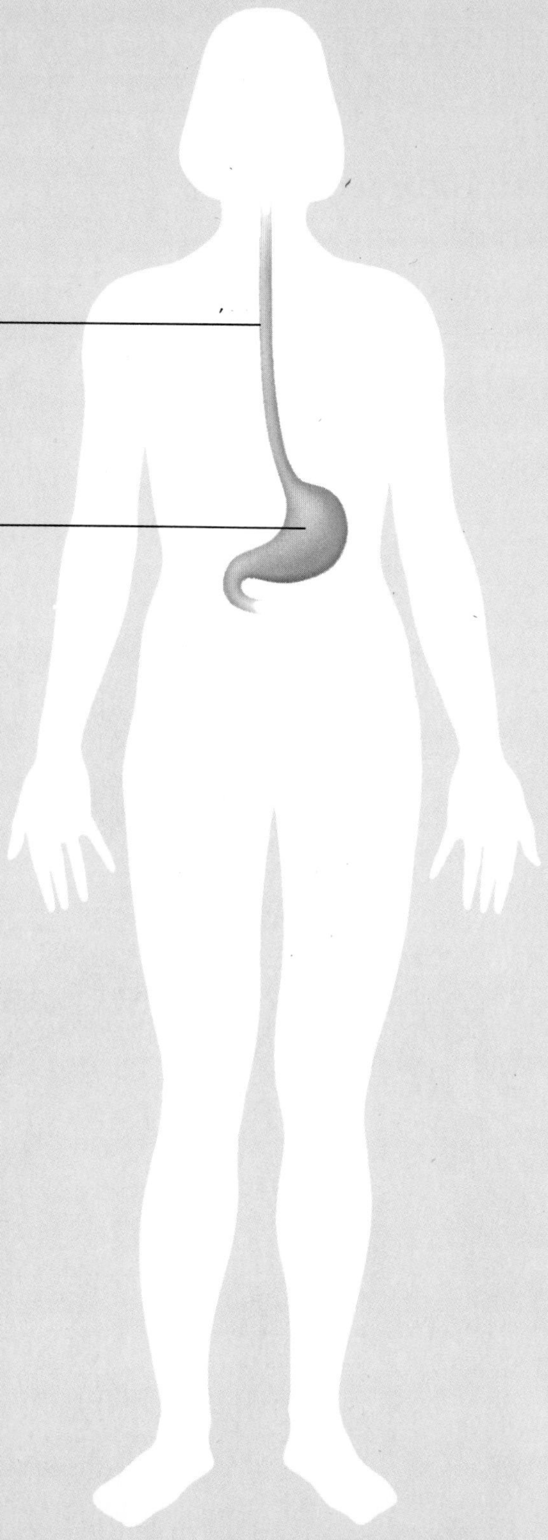

Food tube

Stomach

6 How Do Your Stomach and Intestines Help You?

You must eat food to stay alive. Your body must digest the food you eat so that your cells can use it. When your body digests food, it changes the form of the food.

Food starts to be digested in your mouth. Your teeth and tongue chew up the food. Saliva mixes with the food. Saliva is a juice in your mouth. It helps make food soft enough to swallow.

What happens when you swallow the softened food? This food goes down a long food tube to the stomach. Find this tube in the picture. Muscles in the food tube push the food along.

Stomach juices mix with the food. Stomach muscles turn the food around and around. After a while the food looks like a thick liquid. It is now partly digested.

Soon your stomach squeezes out the thick liquid food into your small intestine. The small intestine is a long narrow tube all curled up inside you. Find it in the picture.

Juices in your small intestine finish digesting the food. The thick liquid food is changed to a thin liquid food. Muscles in your small intestine move the thin liquid along. The thin liquid food with its nutrients moves into blood vessels. These blood vessels are in the sides of your small intestine. Your heart pumps the blood with nutrients to all of your cells.

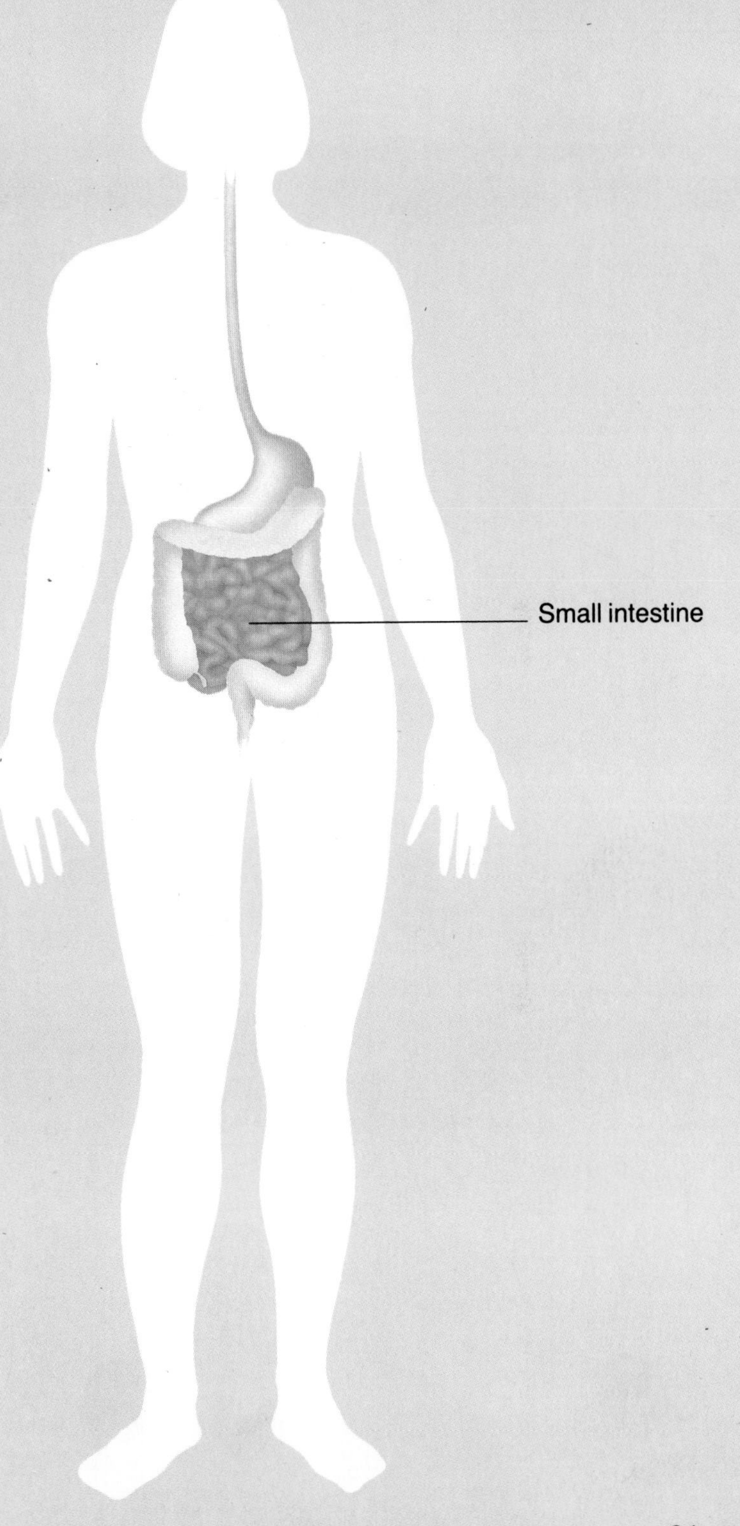

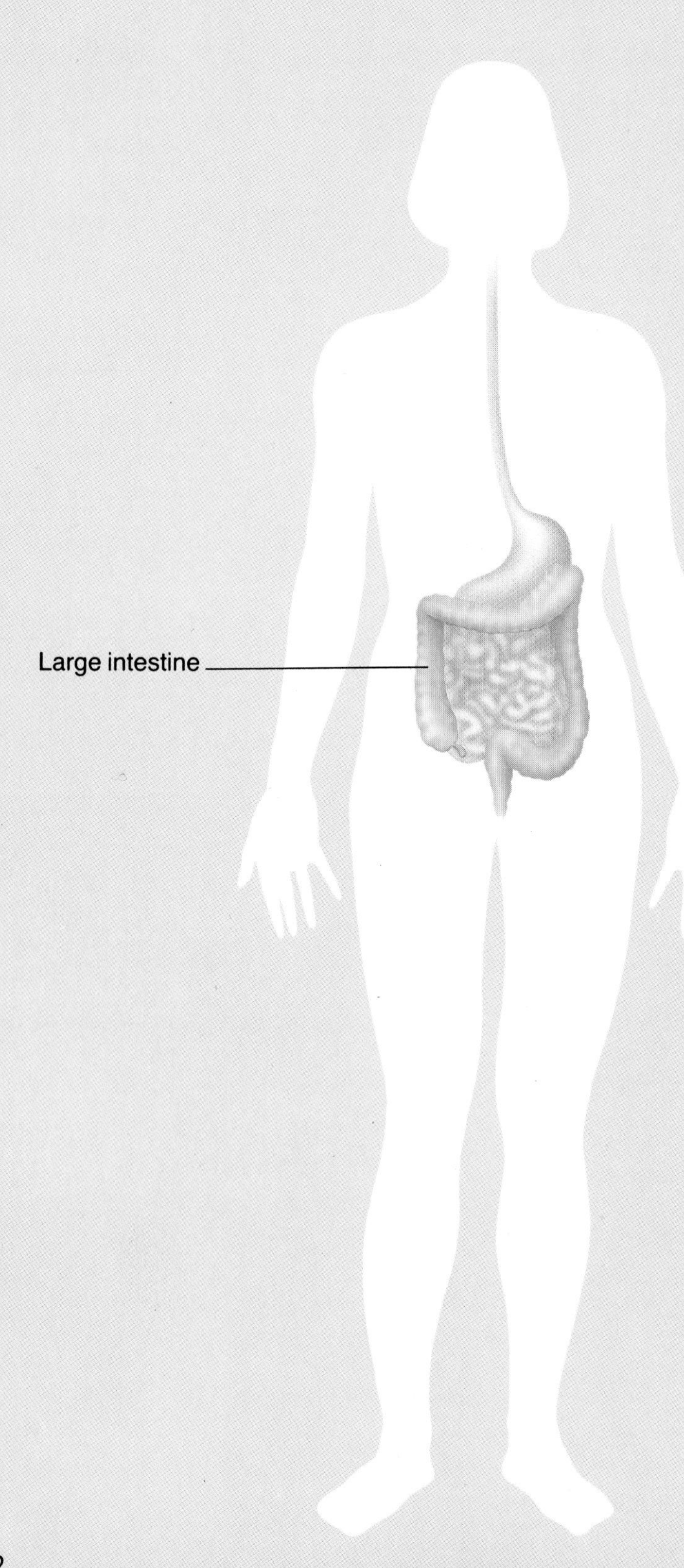

How Does Your Body Get Rid of Food It Cannot Use?

Your body cannot use some parts of the food you eat. For example, your body cannot change fruit skins and seeds to liquid.

Food not used by your body moves from your small intestine to your large intestine. Notice the large intestine in the picture. Your large intestine is a much shorter and wider tube than your small intestine.

In your large intestine, water is removed from food. The parts of the food that are left are wastes. Your body cannot use these wastes. Muscles in your large intestine push the wastes slowly along. After some hours, the wastes are moved out of your body.

The organs that work together to digest food make up a system. Your body has many systems to do different jobs.

Use a finger to trace the path food takes through the body. Start at the mouth and move your finger down the long tube to the stomach. Then move your finger from the stomach to the small intestine. Follow the twists and turns until you reach the large intestine. Trace along the intestine to the place where wastes leave the body.

Think Back

- *See Study Guide on page 227*

1. How do the stomach and small intestine help digest food?
2. What is the path that food takes as it is being digested in the body?

What path does food take in the body?

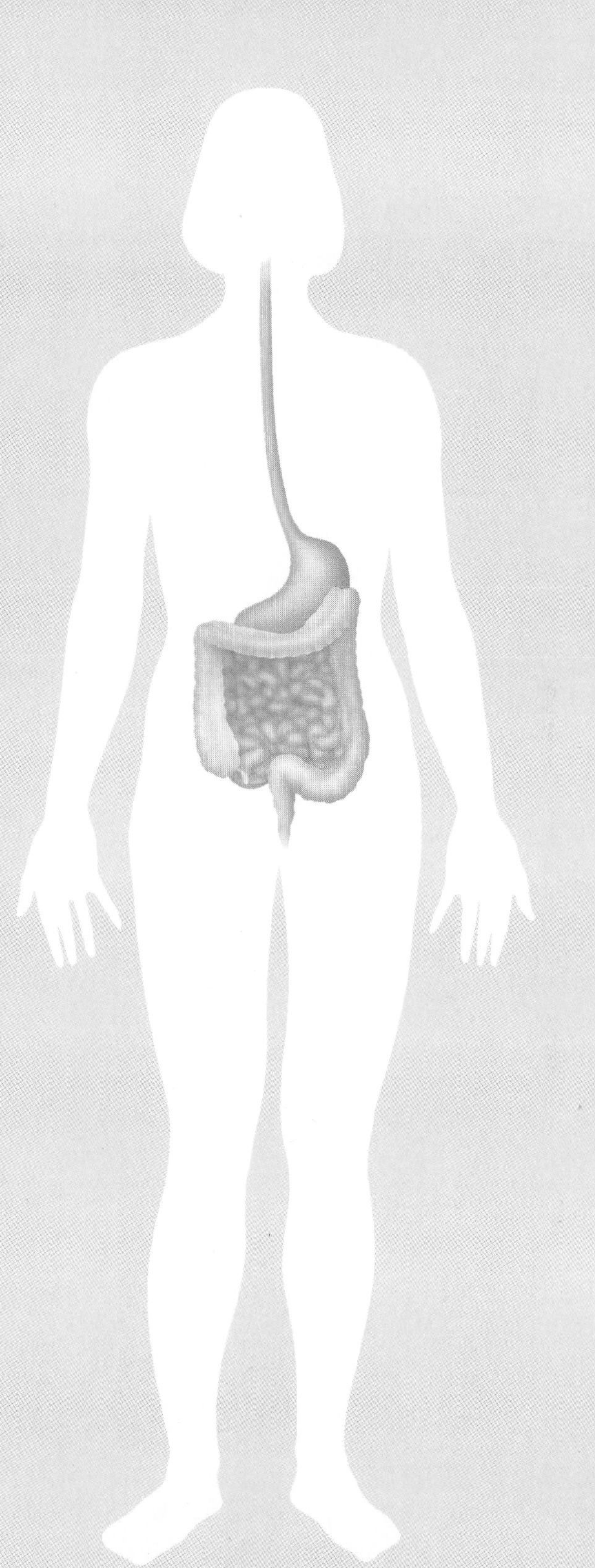

Health Activities Workshop

Finding Out More About Your Brain, Senses, and Heart

1. Find out how your brain works when you try to catch something. Throw a ball up in the air and then catch it. Throw a sheet of paper up in the air. Try to catch it. Throw a ball in the air again. Try catching it with one hand, as the picture shows. Do the same thing with a sheet of paper. Which is easier for your brain to think about catching, the ball or the paper? Explain your answer.

2. Find out where the heart is in the body. Put one end of a cardboard tube against a friend's back. Move the tube around until you find the place where you can hear a heartbeat. You will hear a thumping sound: lub-dup, lub-dup, lub-dup. How many times does your friend's heart beat in one minute?

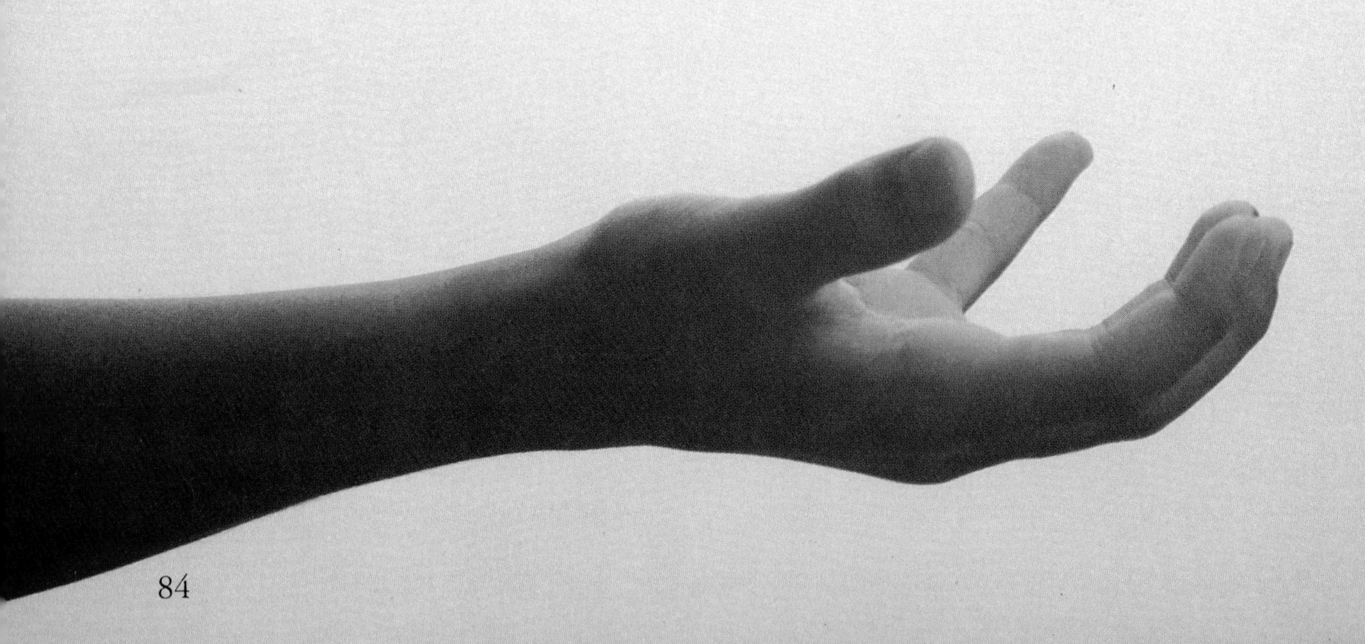

Looking at Careers

3. See how many things a friend can name correctly using the sense of touch. Ask a friend to close his or her eyes. Touch the friend's hand with a sheet of paper, a cotton ball, a soft brush, and a feather.

4. Did you know that pictures can be taken of parts inside your body? A worker called an **X-ray technologist** takes the pictures with an X-ray machine. X-ray machines take pictures of the heart, lungs, and other body organs. They also take pictures of the bones in the body.

An X-ray technologist shows a doctor any X-ray pictures he or she takes. The doctor studies the pictures to see if the body parts are healthy.

Maybe you have had an X-ray picture taken. Explain to the class what happened. You might want to draw "X rays" of parts of the body.

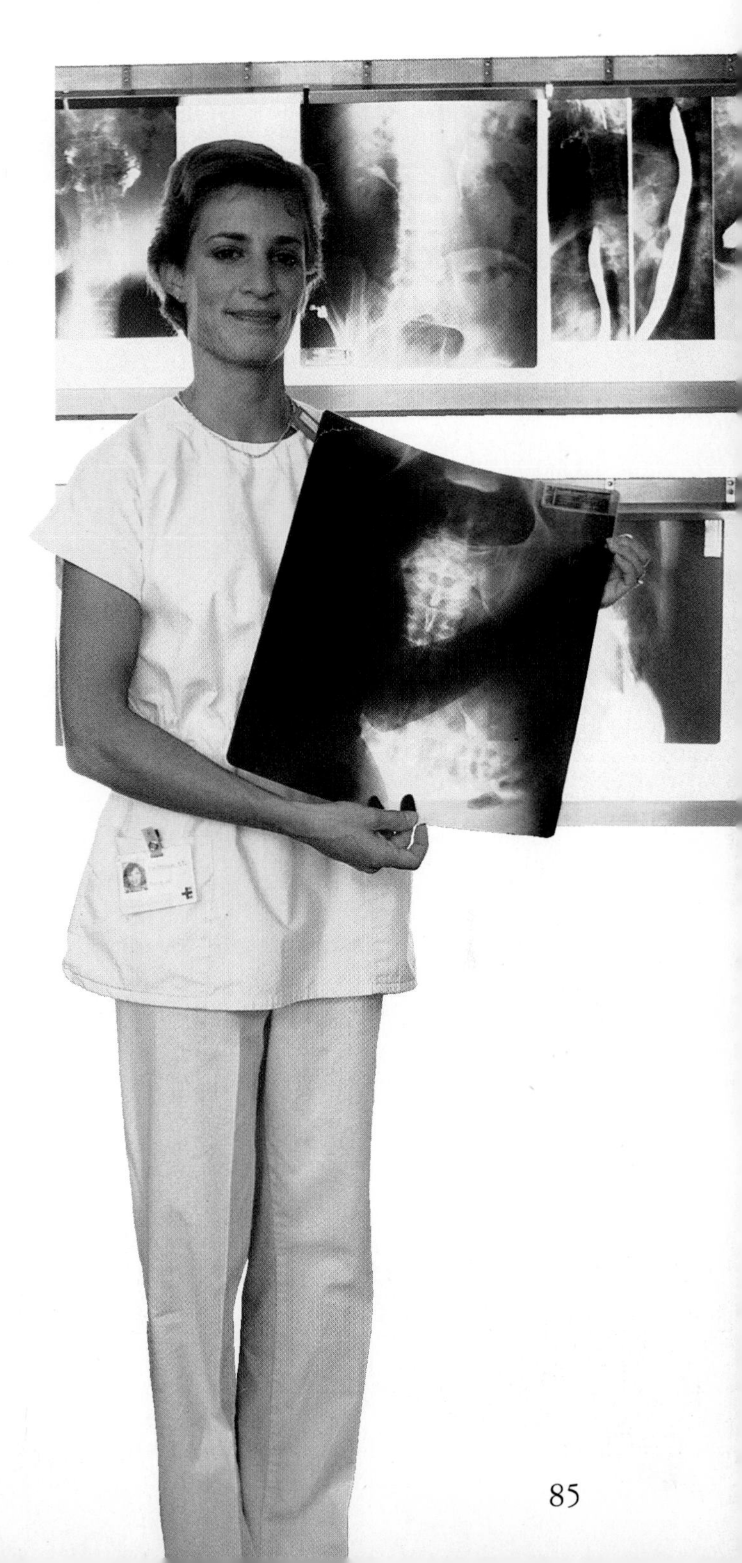

7 How Does Your Body Grow?

Do you know what makes your body grow? You grow because most of your body cells make more cells. Cells grow until they reach a certain size. Then the cells divide to form new cells. For example, bone cells divide to make more bone cells. These new cells also grow and divide. Your body becomes larger as it adds new cells.

You grow in a way that is right for you. No one can tell you exactly how tall someone your age should be. All the children in the picture are the same age, but each is different. Each boy and girl has his or her own way of growing.

You can help yourself grow as you should. Eat healthy foods. Exercise every day to help your muscles get larger and stronger. Get enough sleep each night. Sleep gives your body a chance to rest and grow.

On Your Own
The children in the picture are members of a soccer team. Write a paragraph explaining how playing soccer helps them grow.

Think Back • *Study on your own with Study Guide page 227.*

1. What makes the body grow?
2. What is special about the way a person grows?
3. What can help a person grow as he or she should?

Health Focus

Wilhelm Roentgen's Discovery

About a hundred years ago doctors had no easy way to see inside the body. The only way to see inside was to operate on a patient.

Then in 1895, a German scientist named Wilhelm Roentgen made a wonderful discovery. This scientist discovered X rays. These X rays could pass through the outer layers of the body. The X rays made it possible to see the bones. X-ray pictures gave clear views of the bones.

Today X-ray machines can be used to take pictures of many body parts. X-ray pictures can show the heart, lungs, and other organs. What does this X ray show?

Talk About It

1. What did Wilhelm Roentgen discover?
2. How might Wilhelm Roentgen's discovery help you?

Chapter 3 Review

Reviewing Lesson Objectives

1. Tell what body cells are. (pages 68–69)
2. Tell what muscles and bones do in the body. (pages 70–72)
3. Tell what the brain and nerves do in the body. (pages 74–75)
4. Tell what the heart and blood vessels do. (pages 76–77)
5. Tell what the lungs do. Tell how cells get oxygen and get rid of carbon dioxide. (pages 78–79)
6. Describe the path food takes through the body. (pages 80–83)
7. Explain what makes the body grow. (pages 86–87)

For further review use Study Guide pages 226-227.

Checking Health Vocabulary

Number your paper from 1–11. Match each meaning in Column I with the correct word or words in Column II.

Column I

1. the smallest living part of the body
2. a group of cells that look alike
3. a place where bones fit together
4. a group of different tissues that work together to do the same job
5. a gas in the air people need to stay alive
6. a gas taken away from the cells by the blood
7. a tube through which blood travels in the body
8. change food to a form that the cells in the body can use
9. a juice in the mouth that helps soften food
10. the organ of the body where nutrients in food enter the blood
11. the organ of the body where wastes are passed out of the body

Column II

a. blood vessel
b. carbon dioxide
c. cell
d. digest
e. joint
f. large intestine
g. organ
h. oxygen
i. saliva
j. small intestine
k. tissue

Chapter 3 Test

Complete the Sentence

Number your paper from 1–9. Next to each number write the word that best completes the sentence. Choose the words from the list below.

bones
carbon
cells
heart
nerves
organ
oxygen
small
tissue

1. The body is made of many different kinds of ____.
2. Many bone cells together make up bone ____.
3. Two body parts that work together to move the body are muscles and ____.
4. Messages go to and from the brain over ____.
5. The brain is an ____ made up of different kinds of tissues that work together.
6. Blood picks up the waste gas ____ dioxide from the cells.
7. The ____ pumps blood containing oxygen to the cells.
8. Air breathed into the lungs contains ____.
9. Food is changed to a thin liquid in the ____ intestine.

Short Answer

Number your paper from 10–18. Next to each number write the word or words that best answer the question.

10. What part of a leg lets it move in different ways?
11. What organ do the five senses send messages to?
12. How does the body get rid of carbon dioxide?
13. How does oxygen get from your lungs to your cells?
14. Where does food start to be digested in the body?
15. How does food get from the mouth to the stomach?
16. What happens to food that the body cannot use?
17. What helps the muscles get larger and stronger?
18. What gives the body a chance to rest and grow?

Essay

Write the answers on your paper. Use complete sentences.

19. How would your life be different if you did not have one of your senses?
20. In what ways has your body grown since you were a baby?

Health at Home

Making Up Riddles About the Body

You have learned something about how your body works. You have also learned something about how your body grows. You can have some fun at home by making up riddles for your family to guess. Make up riddles about parts of the body that you have learned about in this chapter. Look at the examples.

When you breathe in, air comes into them. When you breathe out, air goes out of them. What are they?

Every part of you is made up of them. Your body grows because they divide. What are they?

Reading at Home

Heartbeats: Your Body, Your Heart by Alvin and Virginia B. Silverstein. Lippincott, 1983. Learn what the heart does.

Your Five Senses by Ray Broekel. Childrens Press, 1984. Find out how each of your senses helps you.

Chapter **4**

Caring for Your Teeth

What do you think this boy is trying to tell you? He is telling you the number of primary teeth he has lost. How many primary teeth have you lost? How old were you when you lost each tooth? About how old will you be when you lose the rest?

The lessons in this chapter will help answer questions you have about your teeth. One lesson tells the ages at which primary teeth are usually lost. Another lesson tells how your teeth help you. Other lessons tell you how to keep your teeth and gums healthy now and in the future.

1 What Are Some Parts of a Tooth?
2 Why Are Primary Teeth Important?
3 What Can Cause Problems with Teeth and Gums?
4 How Can You Keep Your Teeth and Gums Healthy?
5 What Can Help You Choose Good Products for Tooth Care?

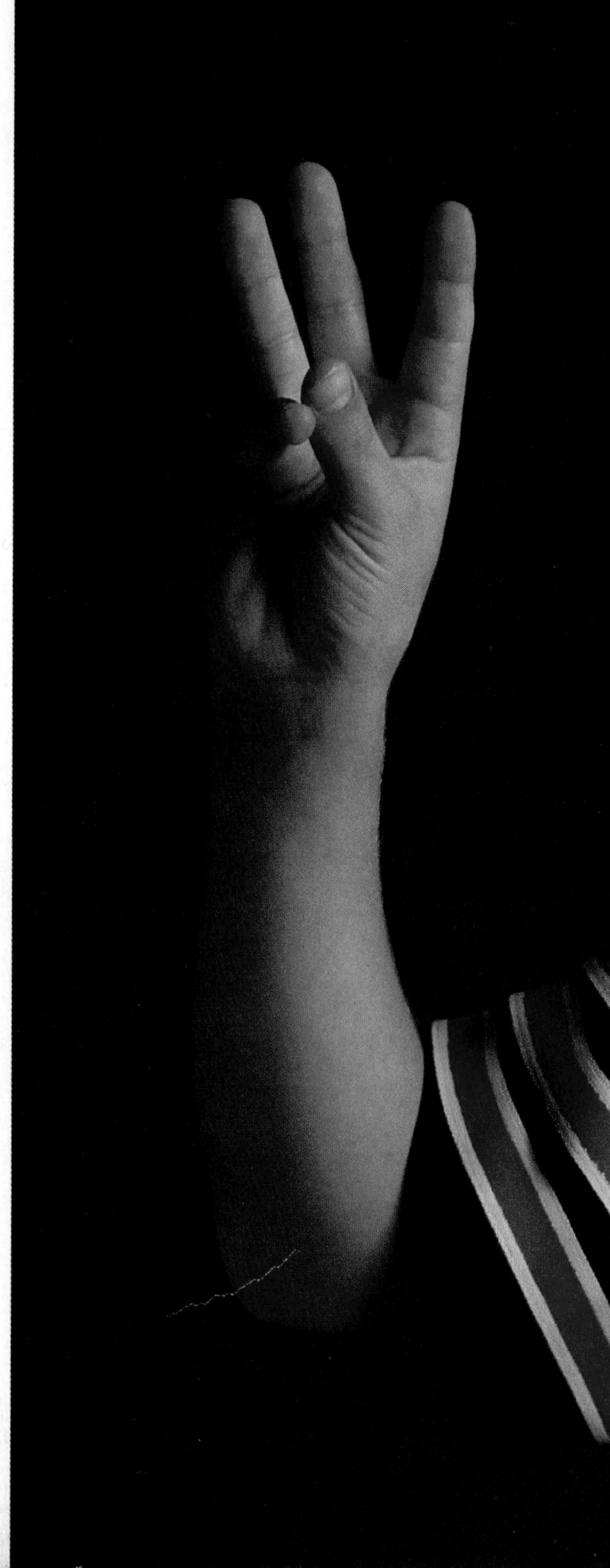

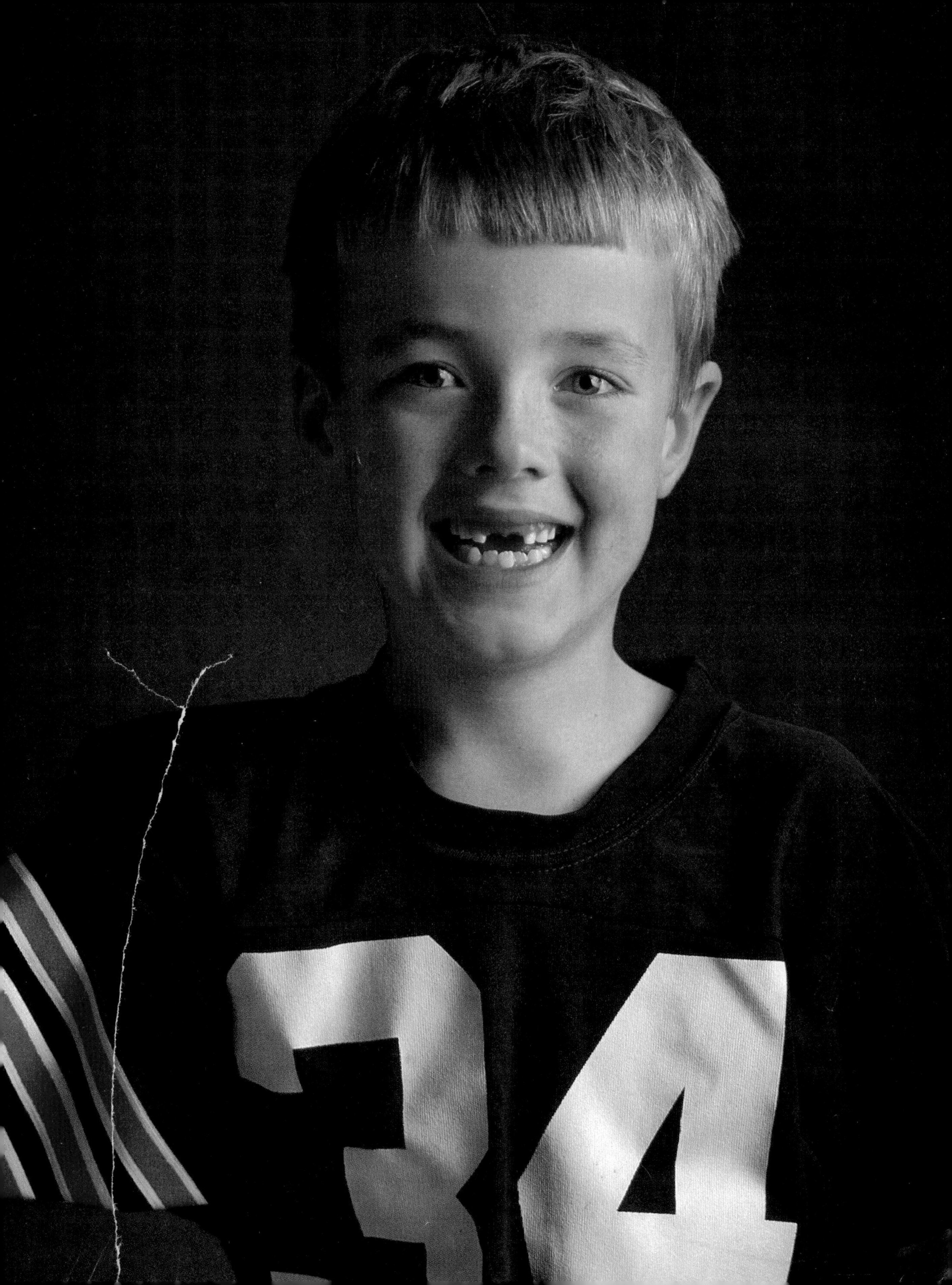
34

crown (kroun), the part of a tooth above the gum.

enamel (i nam′əl), the hard outer covering that protects a tooth.

1 What Are Some Parts of a Tooth?

What do you know about the parts of a tooth? You can see the **crown** and roots of the tooth in the picture on this page. When you look at a tooth in your mouth, you see only its crown. You cannot see the tooth's roots and other parts.

The crown of a tooth is covered by **enamel** as the picture on page 95 shows. This white covering is the hardest material in the body. A tooth's enamel helps protect it from the wear of chewing.

The roots of a tooth are under the gum. The firm, pink tissue around the tooth is the gum. The roots help hold the tooth in the jawbone. Some teeth have one root. Some teeth have two roots. Other teeth have three roots.

The center of a tooth has blood vessels and nerves. Find the blood vessels and nerves in the tooth. Blood in the vessels carries nutrients and oxygen to the tooth. The blood also carries wastes away from the tooth. The nerves send messages from the tooth to the brain. What kind of messages might the nerves send?

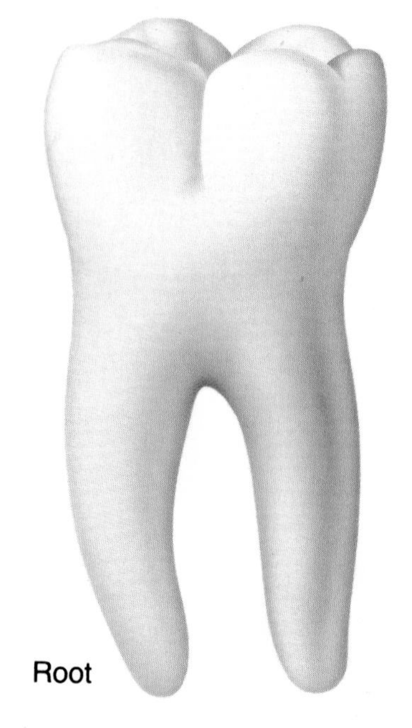

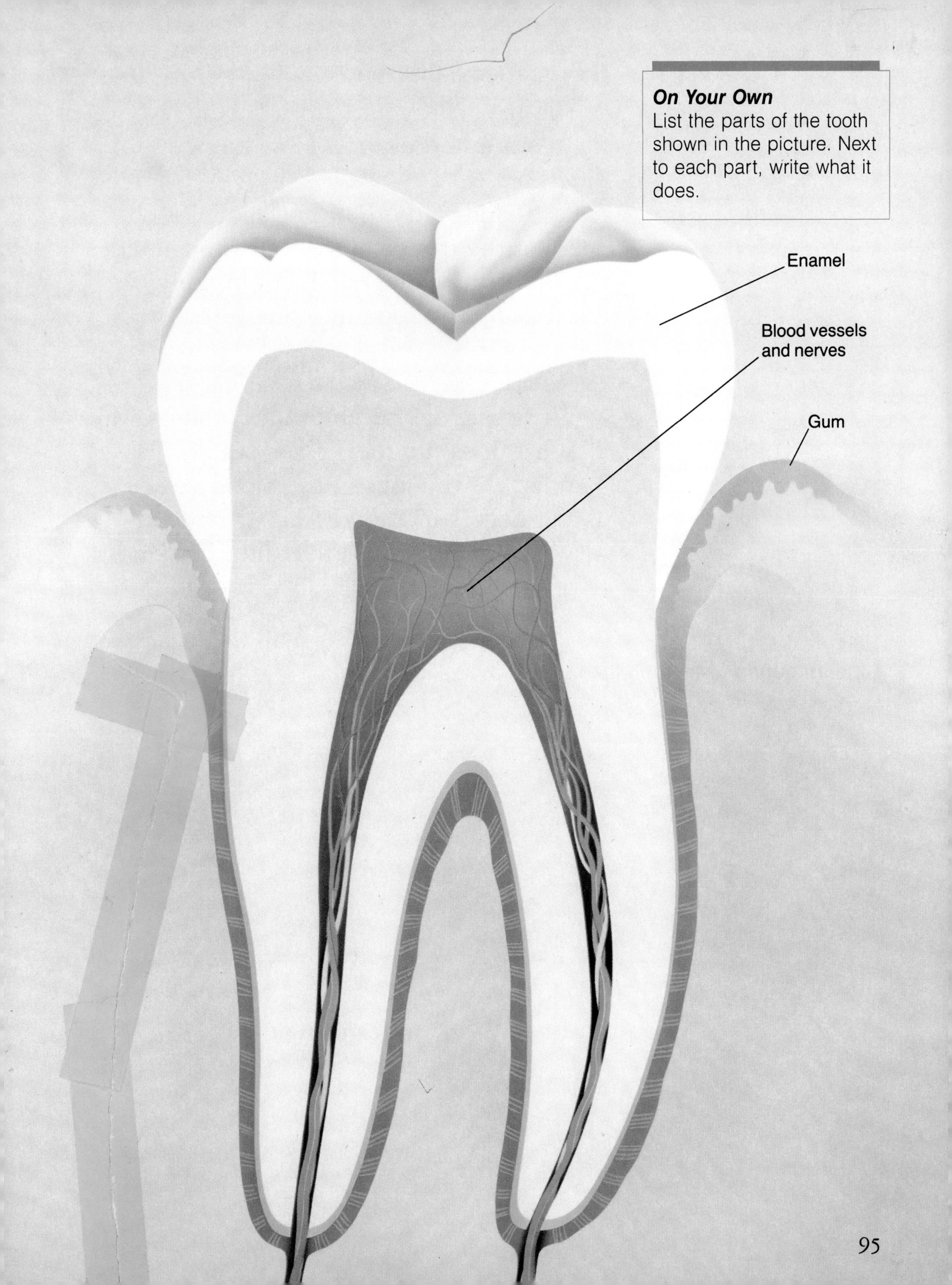

On Your Own
List the parts of the tooth shown in the picture. Next to each part, write what it does.

How Are Teeth Different?

You have different kinds of teeth. Notice the teeth in the picture. How are they different?

Each kind of tooth does a special job. Teeth at the front and sides of your mouth cut and tear food apart. Teeth in the back crush and grind food into bits.

Think Back • *Study on your own with Study Guide page 228.*

1. What part of a tooth protects the crown?
2. What does the root of a tooth do?
3. What are the jobs of the blood vessels and nerves in a tooth?
4. What are some jobs that different kinds of teeth do?

Different kinds of teeth in the mouth

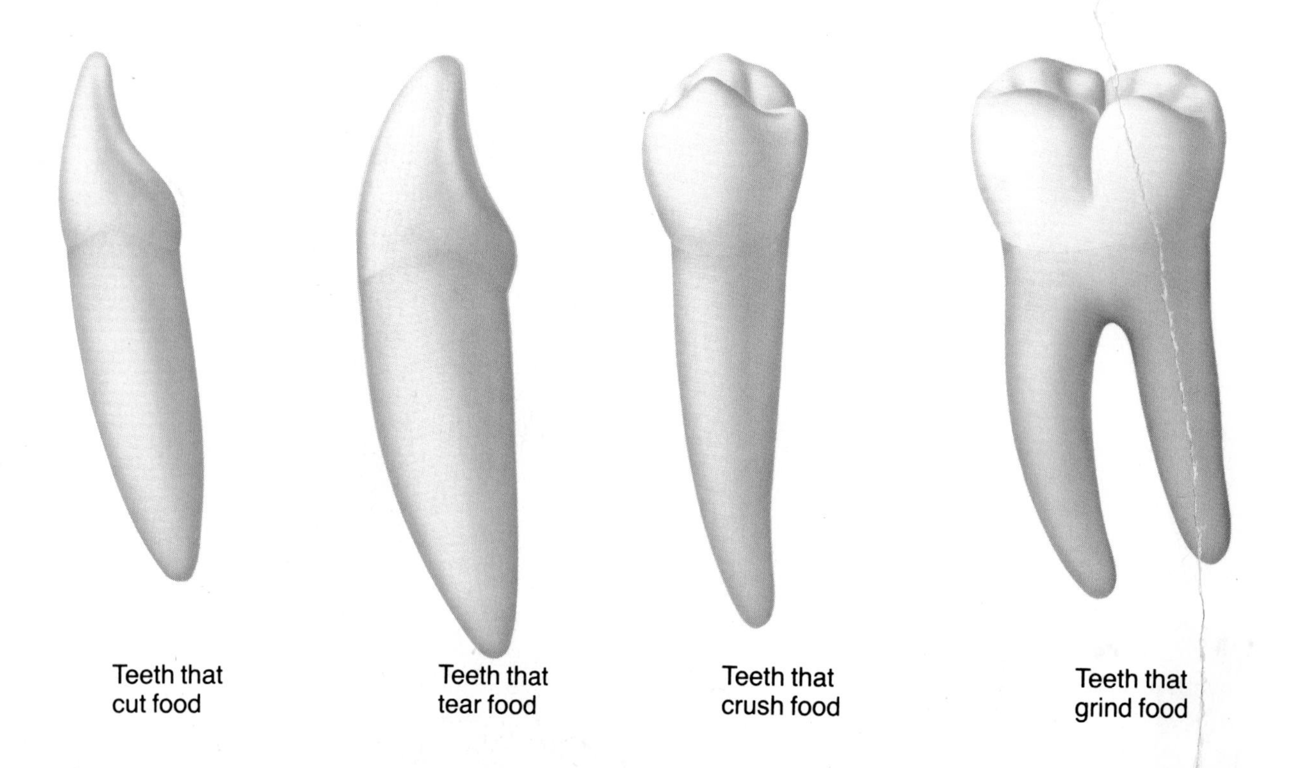

Health Activities Workshop

Learning More About Your Teeth

1. Draw a picture that shows important parts of a tooth, inside and out. Next to each part, write its name.

2. Find the different kinds of teeth in your mouth. Look at your teeth in a mirror as shown. Find the eight teeth with flat edges. Four of these are top teeth and four are bottom teeth. Next find the two top teeth and the two bottom teeth with sharp points. Then look for four top teeth and four bottom teeth with rounded edges.

primary (prī′mer′ē) **teeth,** first twenty teeth that come through a child's gums.

permanent (pėr′mə nənt) **teeth,** the second set of teeth.

2 Why Are Primary Teeth Important?

You will grow just two sets of teeth. Right now you have some teeth in your mouth from your first set. You should take good care of the teeth until they are ready to come out.

Your first set of teeth is made up of twenty **primary teeth.** Most babies are born without teeth. You were probably about six months old when you got your first tooth. By the time you were three, you had all of your primary teeth.

Your primary teeth help you in many ways. Primary teeth help shape your face. They help you chew your food. They help you speak clearly. Primary teeth also hold space open so your second set of teeth can come in straight.

Try to take care of your primary teeth. Good care can help keep your primary teeth from coming out too soon. The picture shows about how old you will be when you lose each primary tooth.

Your **permanent teeth** are your second set of teeth. Maybe you first lost a primary tooth at age six or seven. A permanent tooth soon appeared to take its place. In time a permanent tooth will replace each of your primary teeth. Your permanent teeth can last all your life if you take care of them.

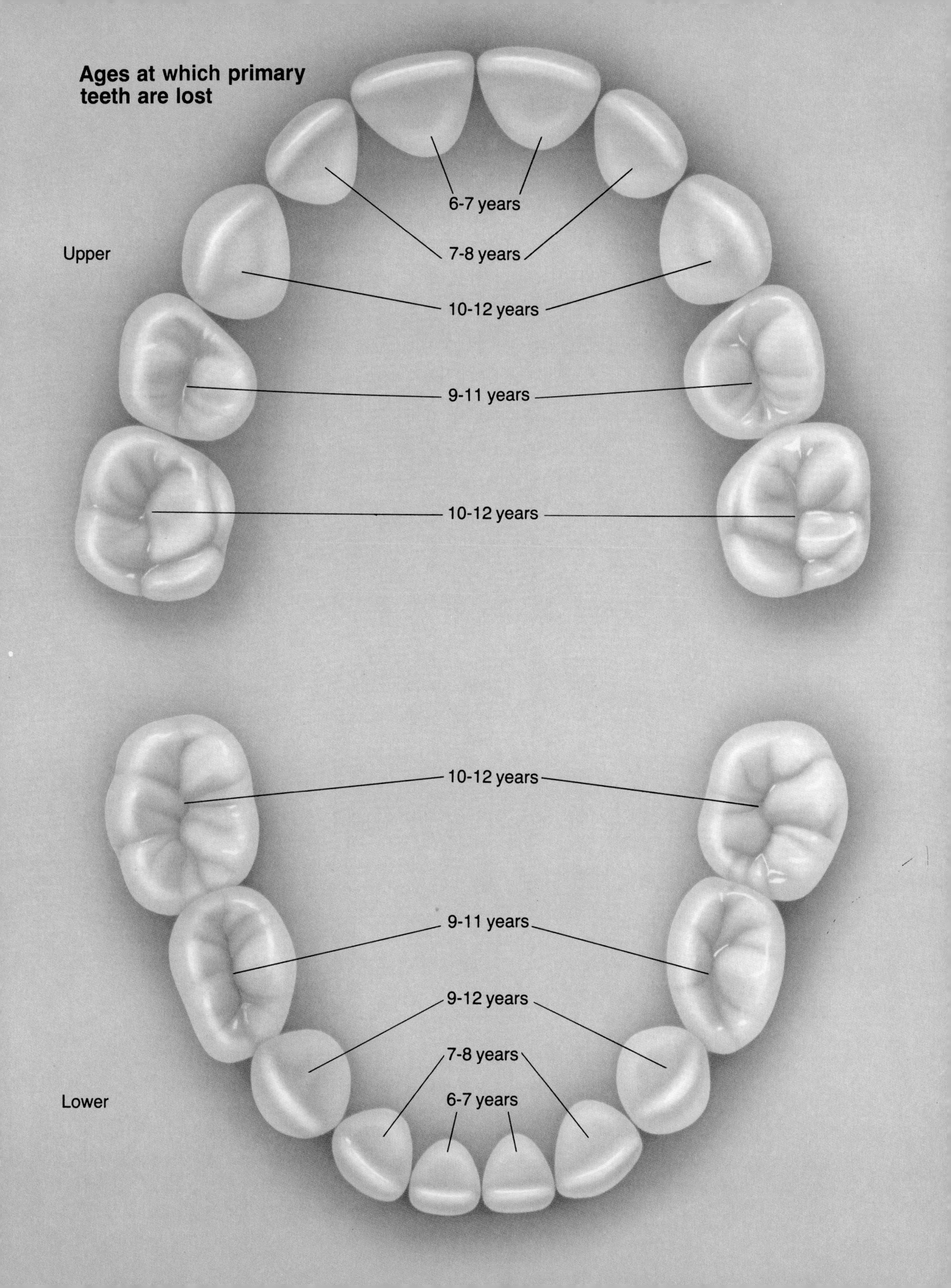
Ages at which primary teeth are lost
Upper
6-7 years
7-8 years
10-12 years
9-11 years
10-12 years
10-12 years
9-11 years
9-12 years
7-8 years
6-7 years
Lower

What Can Help Permanent Teeth Come in Straight?

Suppose a primary tooth comes out too soon. It leaves an empty space. The teeth on each side of the empty space might tip toward the space. The permanent tooth might not have enough room to grow in. It will grow in crooked.

The picture shows an open space after a primary tooth came out too soon. The primary teeth on both sides have tipped toward each other. What will happen to the permanent tooth as it grows in the space?

The permanent tooth does not have enough room to grow in straight.

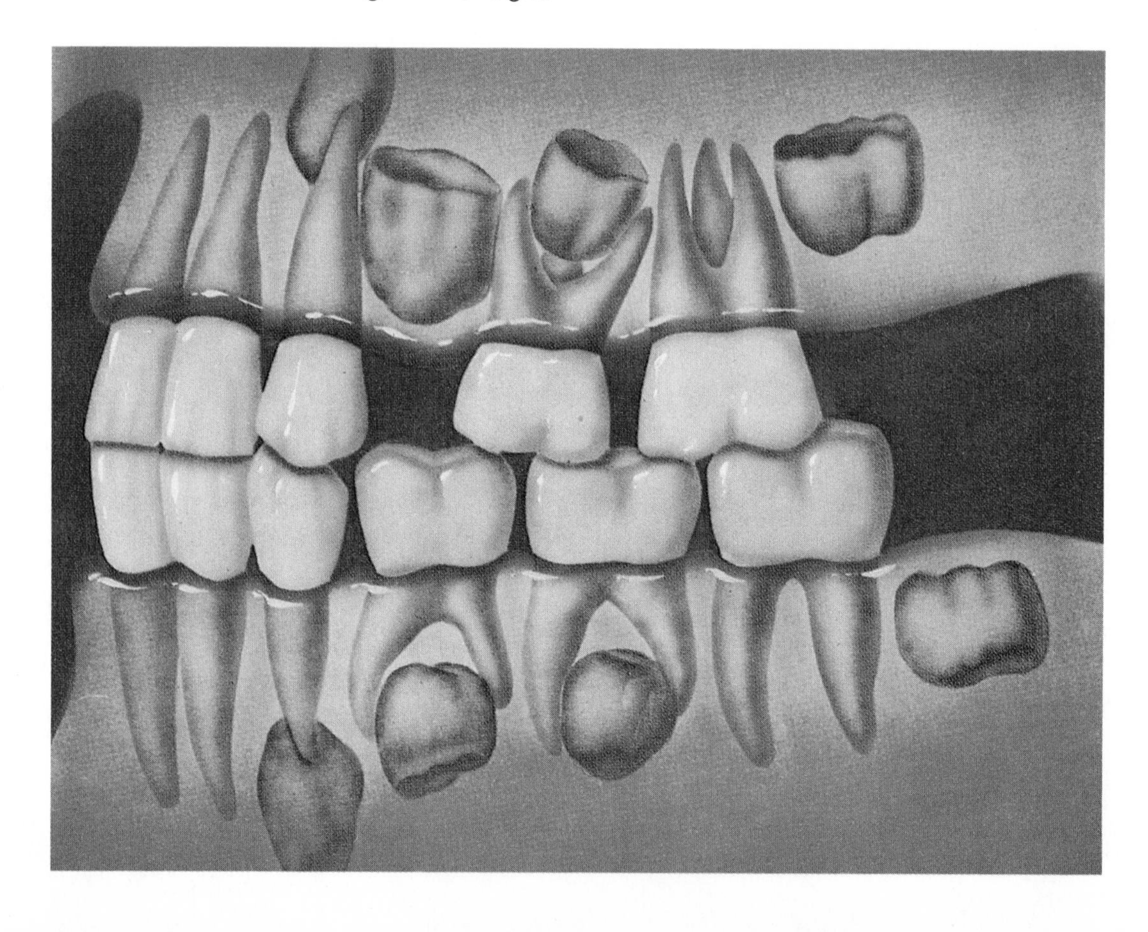

A dentist can keep primary teeth from moving out of place. The dentist uses the space maintainer you see in the picture. The space maintainer is made of wire. The maintainer holds a space open for the permanent tooth that will grow in later. Then the permanent tooth will have a better chance of growing in straight.

Think Back • *Study on your own with Study Guide page 228.*

1. What are the jobs of primary teeth?
2. What can happen if a primary tooth comes out too soon?
3. How can a dentist help keep primary teeth from moving out of place?

Space maintainer

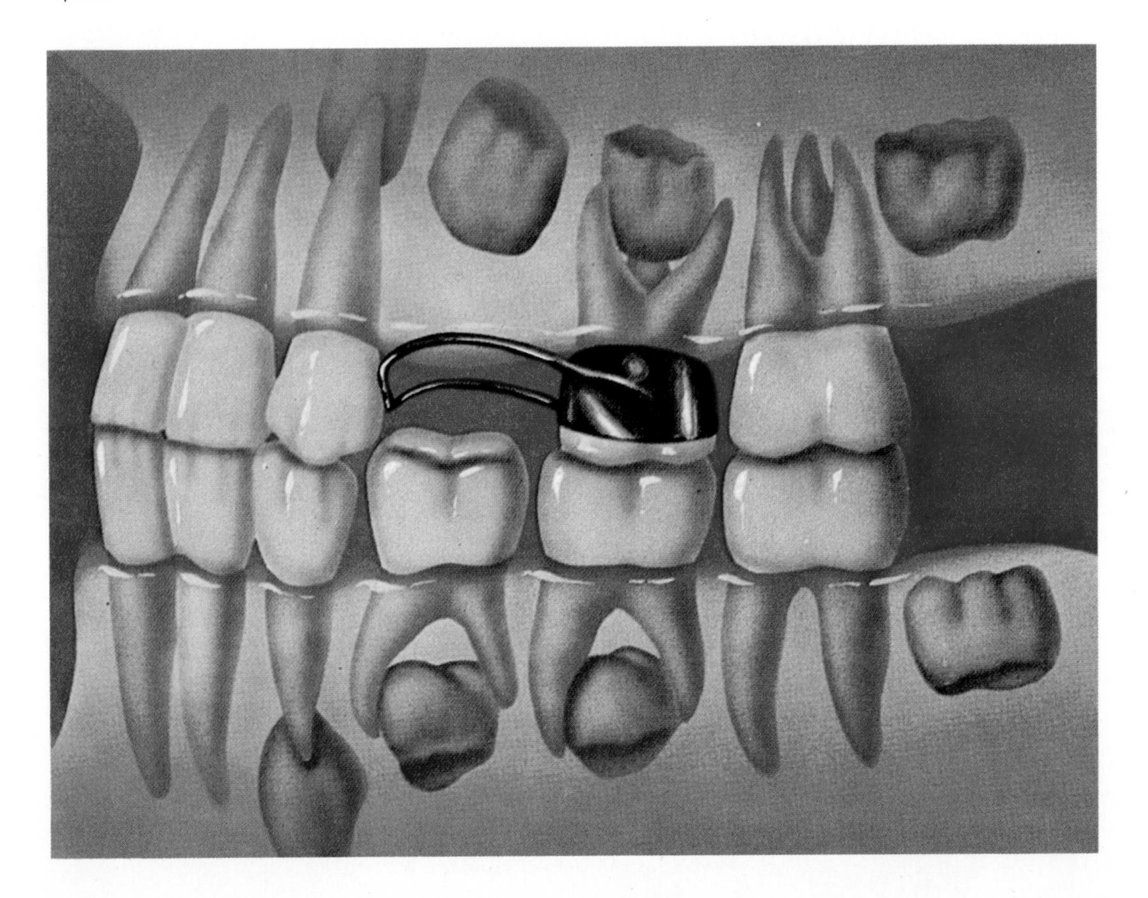

plaque (plak), a sticky material made up of germs.

cavity (kav′ə tē), a hole in a tooth caused by acid.

3 What Can Cause Problems with Teeth and Gums?

Bumping a tooth on something hard can hurt a tooth. **Plaque** can also hurt a tooth. Plaque is a sticky covering of harmful germs. Plaque is always forming on your teeth and between them. You cannot see plaque but it can still be there.

Many of the foods you eat have sugar in them. The germs in plaque use the sugar to make an acid. In time, this acid can make a hole in a tooth. A hole in a tooth is a **cavity.** You can see a tooth cavity in the picture.

Cavity in a tooth

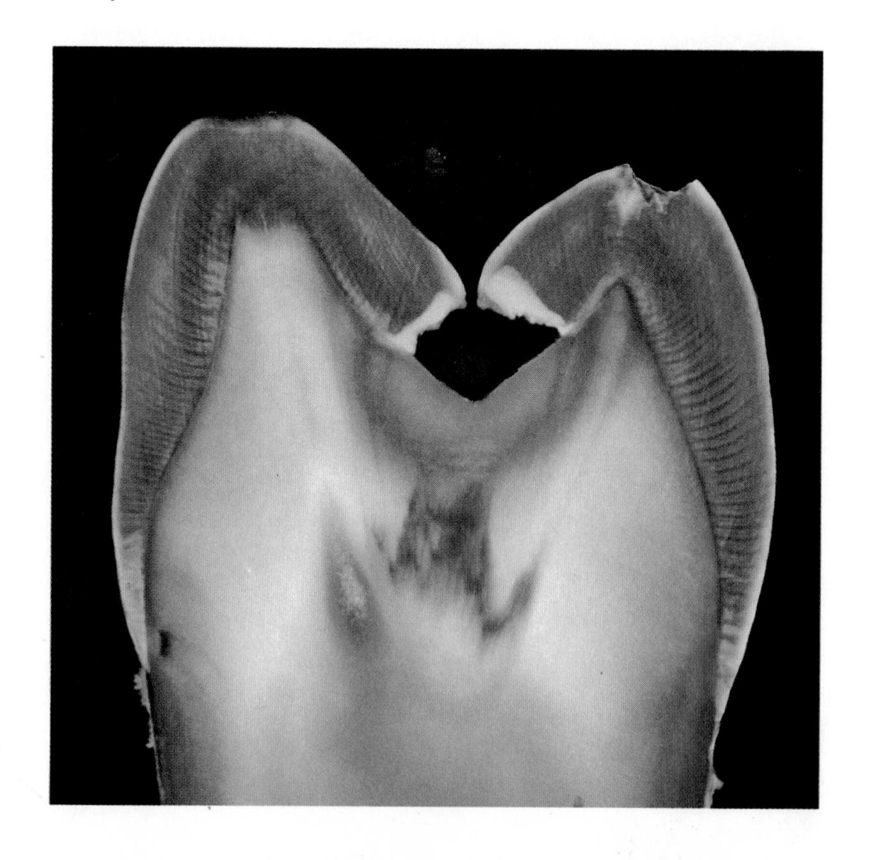

Plaque can hurt gums as well as teeth. Gum disease begins when plaque builds up where the teeth and gums meet. The picture shows where plaque can build up on teeth. The acid in the plaque harms the gums. If you have gum disease, your gums might bleed when you brush your teeth.

Did You Know?
Once harmful acids form in the mouth, they can attack the teeth for about twenty minutes.

Think Back • *Study on your own with Study Guide page 228.*

1. How can plaque hurt a tooth?
2. What is a cavity?
3. How does plaque harm gums?

The green dye shows where plaque has built up on these teeth.

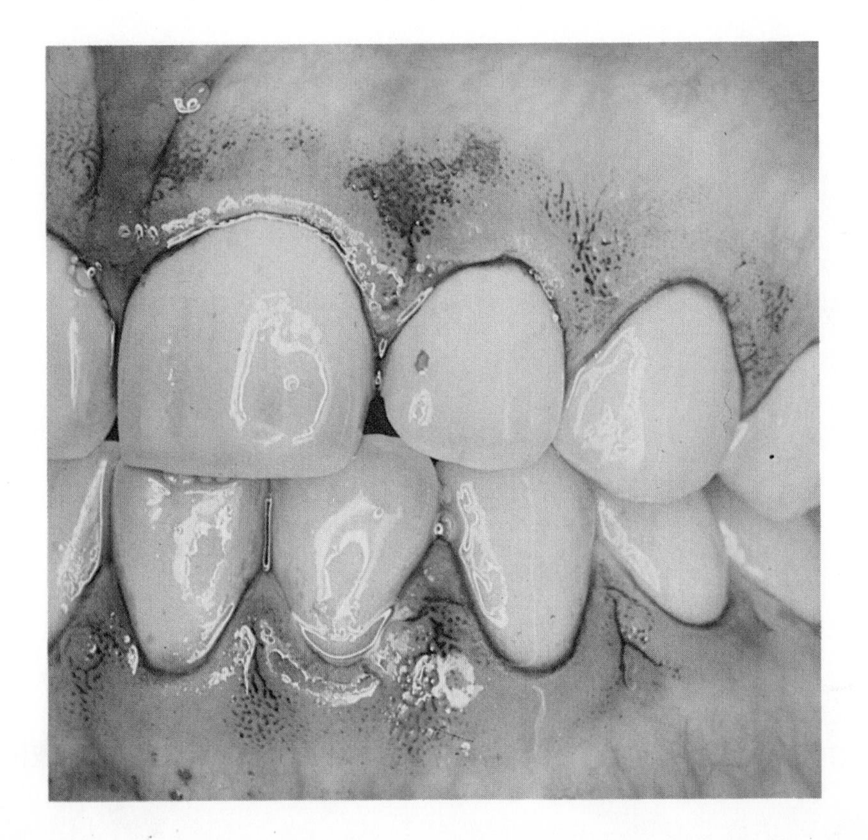

> ***Did You Know?***
> Brushing your tongue will help keep your breath fresh. You should brush your tongue very gently.

4 How Can You Keep Your Teeth and Gums Healthy?

Brushing your teeth helps prevent cavities. You should try to brush your teeth at least once a day. Bedtime is a good time to brush your teeth. Also brush your teeth after eating if you can. Brushing helps remove plaque and bits of food from your teeth and gums.

The pictures show some good ways to brush your teeth. Hold the toothbrush alongside the teeth. Tip the brush back against the gum line as the picture shows. Brush back and forth, back and forth. Brush the outsides and the insides of your teeth. Use short strokes. How will you brush the insides of your front teeth?

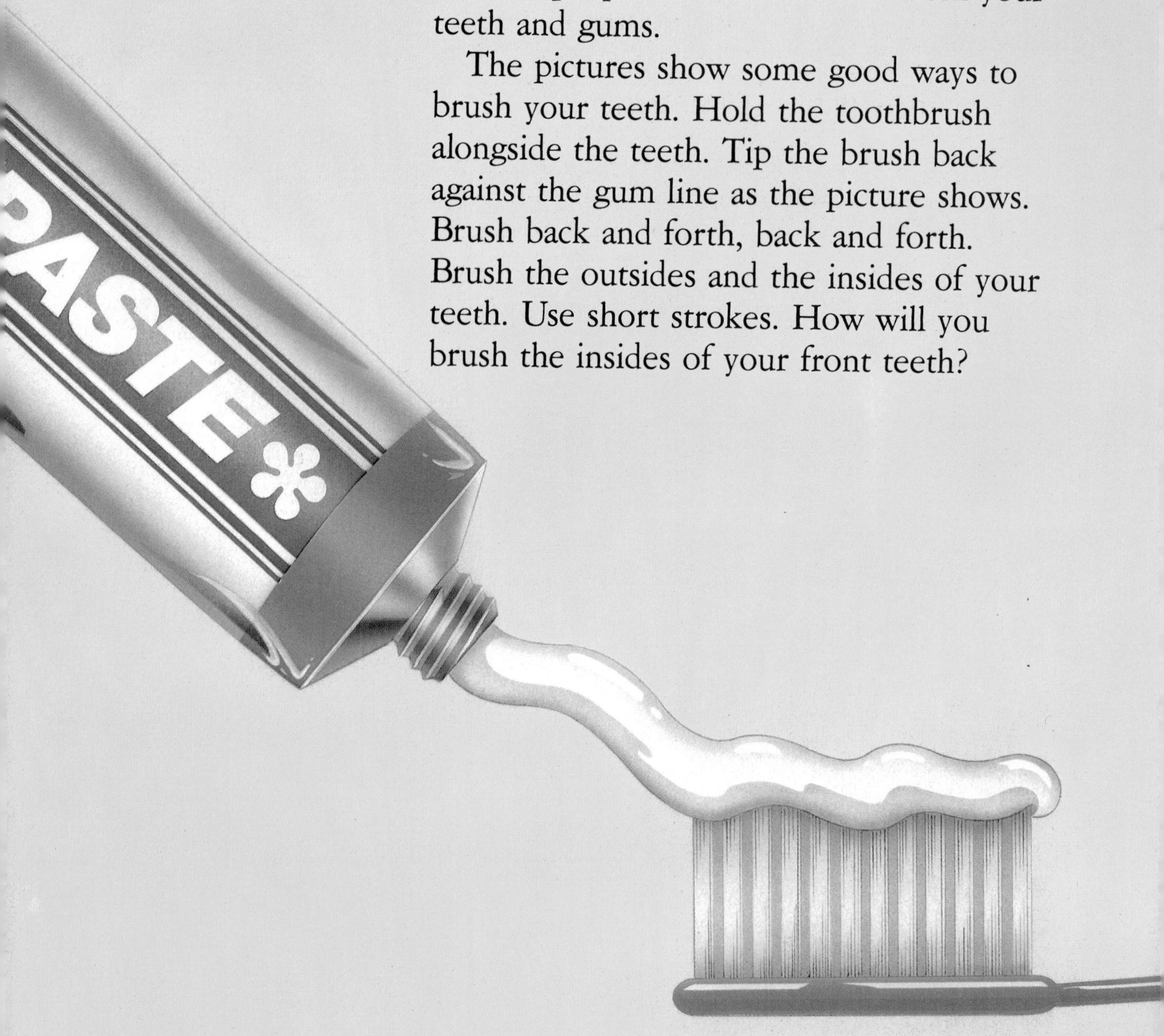

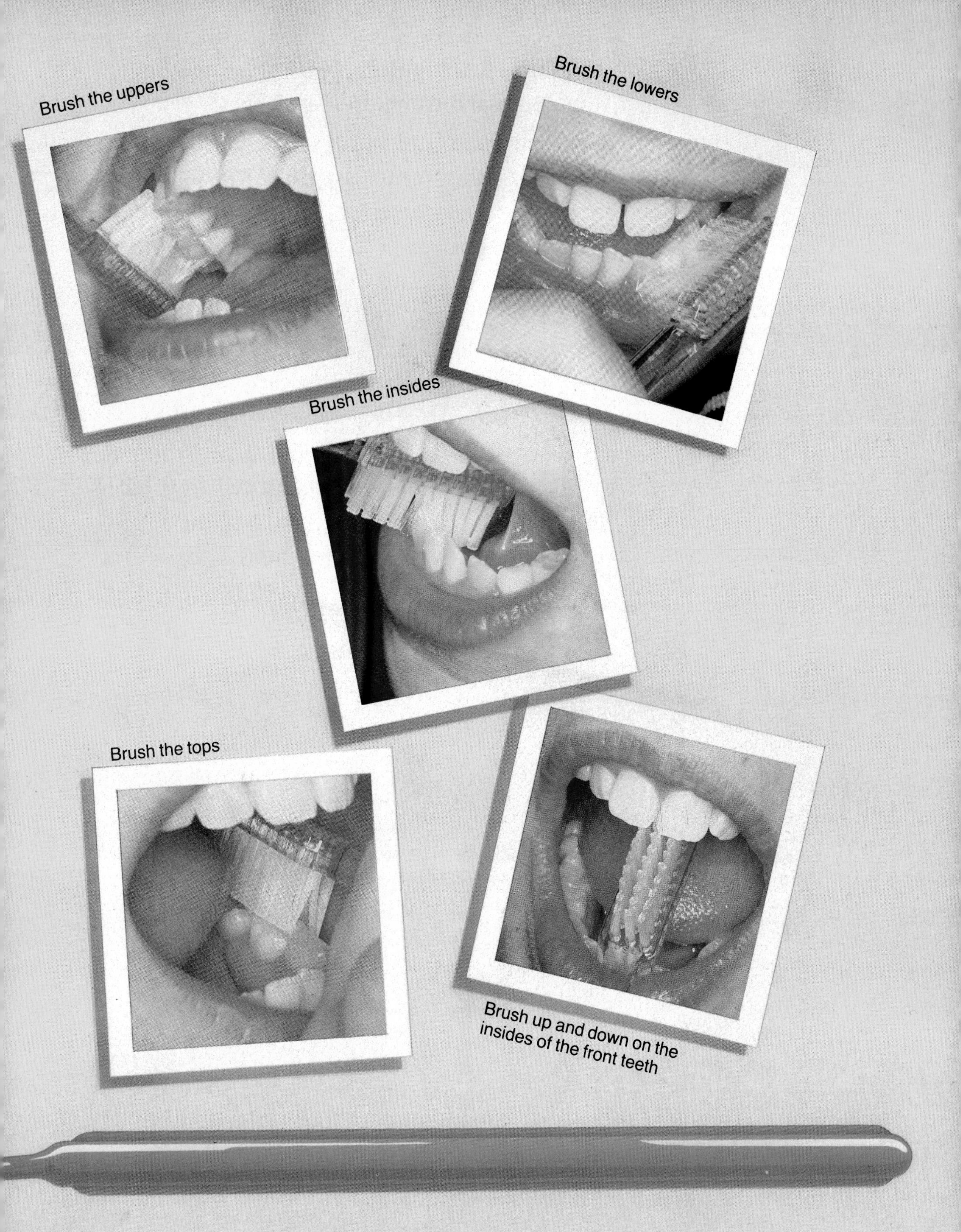
Brush the uppers
Brush the lowers
Brush the insides
Brush the tops
Brush up and down on the insides of the front teeth

How Can Flossing Help Keep Your Teeth and Gums Healthy?

Flossing can help prevent cavities in your teeth. Flossing removes plaque and bits of food from between your teeth and near your gum line. It helps keep plaque from harming your gums.

The boy shown here has asked his mother for help in flossing his teeth. She has carefully placed dental floss between two of his teeth. Next, she will gently move the dental floss up and down the side of each tooth. Gentle flossing will not harm the gums. You might want to ask an adult in your family to help you floss your teeth.

This mother is helping her son floss his teeth.

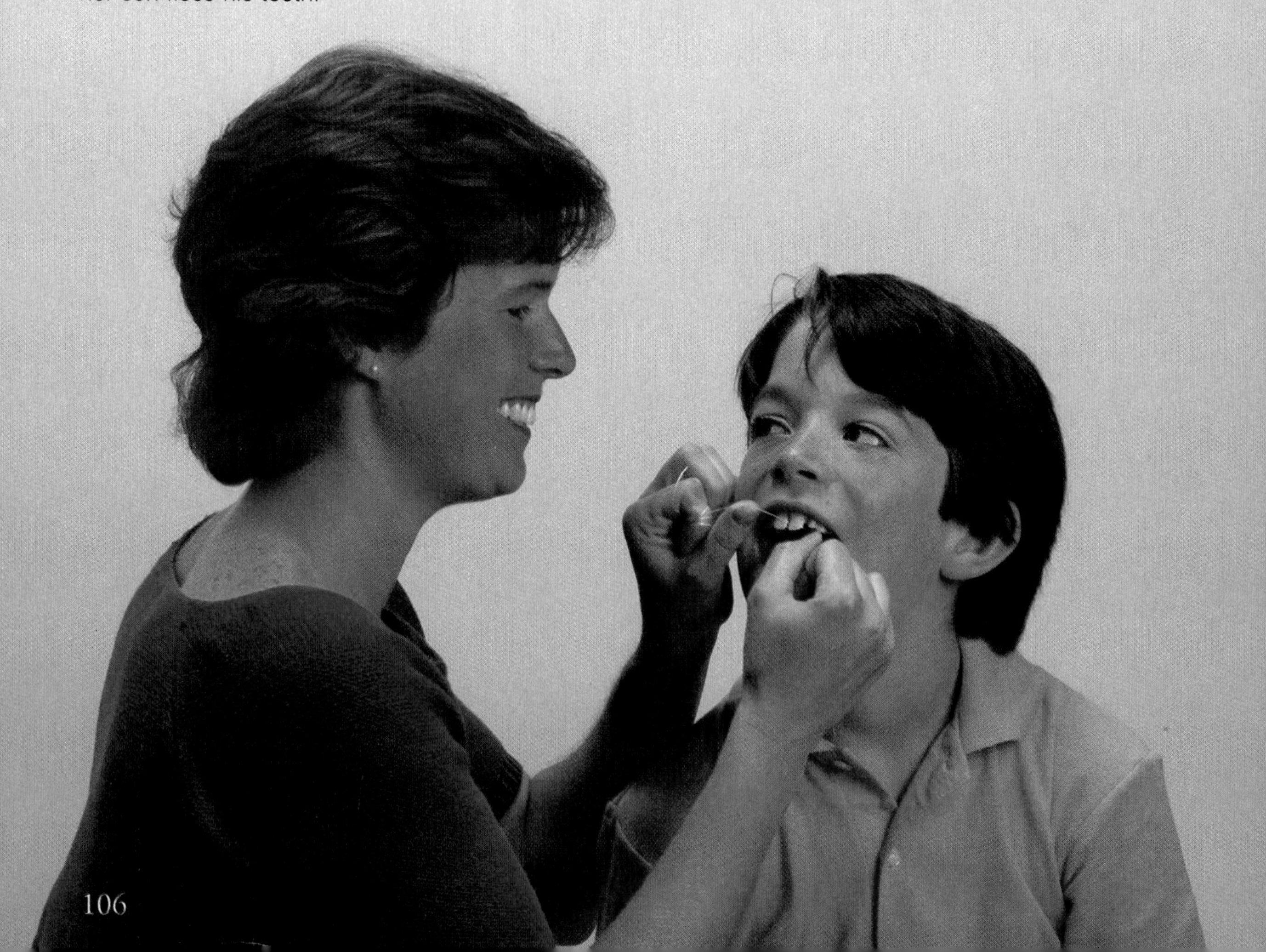

What Kinds of Foods Can Help Keep Your Teeth and Gums Healthy?

Eat foods from the four food groups each day to help keep your teeth and gums healthy. What foods from the four food groups do you see in the picture?

Try not to eat too many sweet, sticky foods. Caramels, cookies, pies, and cakes are all sweet, sticky foods. Sugar in these foods can stick to your teeth. If you do not brush right away, the sugar can cause cavities.

Suppose you chew gum. What kind of gum can you chew to not harm your teeth?

How Does a Dentist Help Keep Your Teeth and Gums Healthy?

If you can, visit a dentist as often as he or she tells you. The dentist has special tools to clean your teeth. Sometimes a dental hygienist works in the dentist's office. The dental hygienist can also clean your teeth.

Even if you brush and floss, some plaque might stay on your teeth and harden. The plaque can cause gum disease. You cannot get the plaque off by yourself. The dentist uses special tools to clean the plaque off your teeth.

If the dentist finds a cavity, he or she fills it. Look at the pictures. How does a dentist fill a cavity?

Think Back • *Study on your own with Study Guide page 229.*

1. How can brushing and flossing help keep teeth and gums healthy?
2. What kinds of foods help keep teeth and gums healthy?
3. How does a dentist help keep teeth and gums healthy?

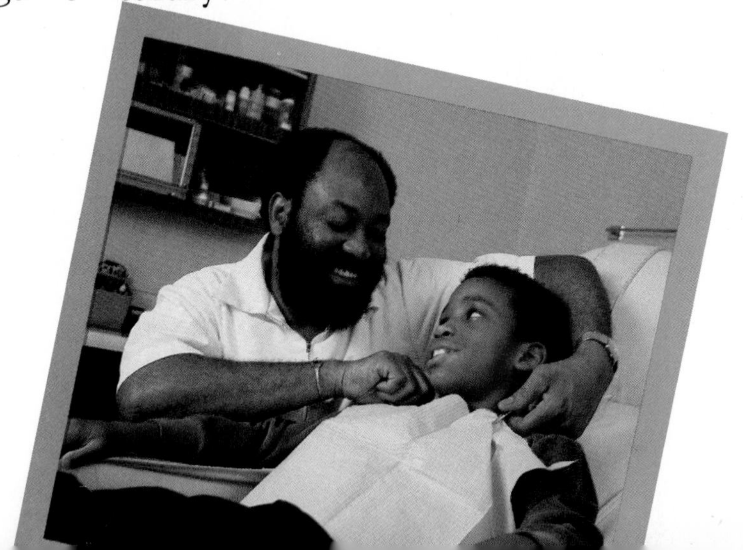

This dentist is getting ready to fill a cavity in the boy's tooth.

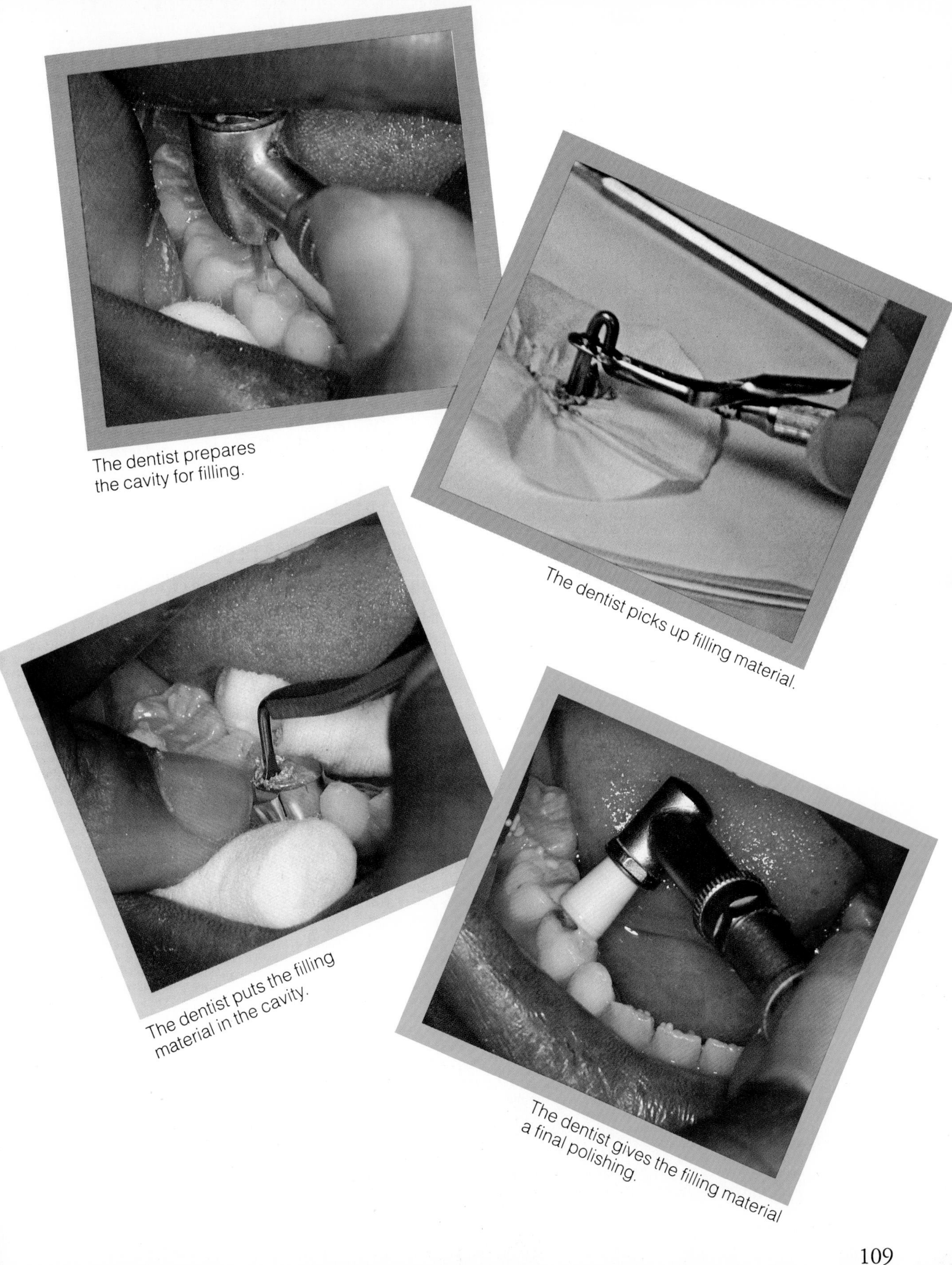

The dentist prepares the cavity for filling.

The dentist picks up filling material.

The dentist puts the filling material in the cavity.

The dentist gives the filling material a final polishing.

Keeping Teeth and Gums Healthy

1. You cannot do a good job of cleaning your teeth if your toothbrush is worn out. The picture shows how the brush part of your toothbrush should look. Check your toothbrush at home to see if the brush part is worn out. Tell what you might do about your toothbrush if it is worn out.

2. Unscramble these words. Each word has to do with tooth care. Write the unscrambled words on your own paper.

fsoslnig
rbuhsnig
oothtrbuhs
denalt yhgeinsti

3. Draw pictures of foods that help keep your teeth and gums healthy. Cut the pictures out and paste them on paper to make a design. Put a title on your design such as "Foods to Help Keep Teeth and Gums Healthy."

Looking at Careers

4. A **dental hygienist** works in a dentist's office. She or he uses special tools to clean teeth. A dental hygienist also takes X rays of teeth.

Pretend that you are a dental hygienist working in a dentist's office. Act out what a dental hygienist does. What did you like and not like about being a hygienist?

5 What Can Help You Choose Good Products for Tooth Care?

What can an advertisement do? An ad can tell many things about a product. For example, an ad might tell how to use the product. The ad might also tell what is in the product and how much it costs. What does this toothpaste ad say?

You might see many ads for toothpastes. Most of them say that they help prevent cavities. What can help you decide which toothpaste to choose?

You can ask dentists or dental hygienists for advice. They will probably tell you to look on a toothpaste box or tube. Look for a special seal. It is the ADA seal you see in the picture. ADA stands for the American Dental Association. The ADA puts its seal on toothpastes that help prevent cavities. Look for the ADA seal when you are choosing a toothpaste.

On Your Own
Make up an advertisement for a toothpaste. Be sure your ad has information about the ADA seal.

How Can You Decide Which Products Are Right for You?

You can ask your dentist or dental hygienist for advice if you need a new toothbrush. Either one can tell you what kind of toothbrush you should use. Then you will be able to choose the toothbrush that is right for you.

Use a toothbrush that is the right size for your mouth. The brush part of the toothbrush should be small enough to reach each of your teeth. The brush should be soft with rounded edges. The top of the toothbrush should be flat, as the pictures show.

This boy's toothbrush is the right size for his mouth.

You also can ask your dentist which kind of dental floss you should use. You can choose waxed or unwaxed dental floss, as the picture shows. You might find waxed floss easier to use if your teeth are close together.

Think Back • *Study on your own with Study Guide page 229.*

1. What might an advertisement tell about a product for tooth care?
2. What does the ADA seal on a toothpaste tell about the toothpaste?
3. Who can help people choose good products for tooth care?

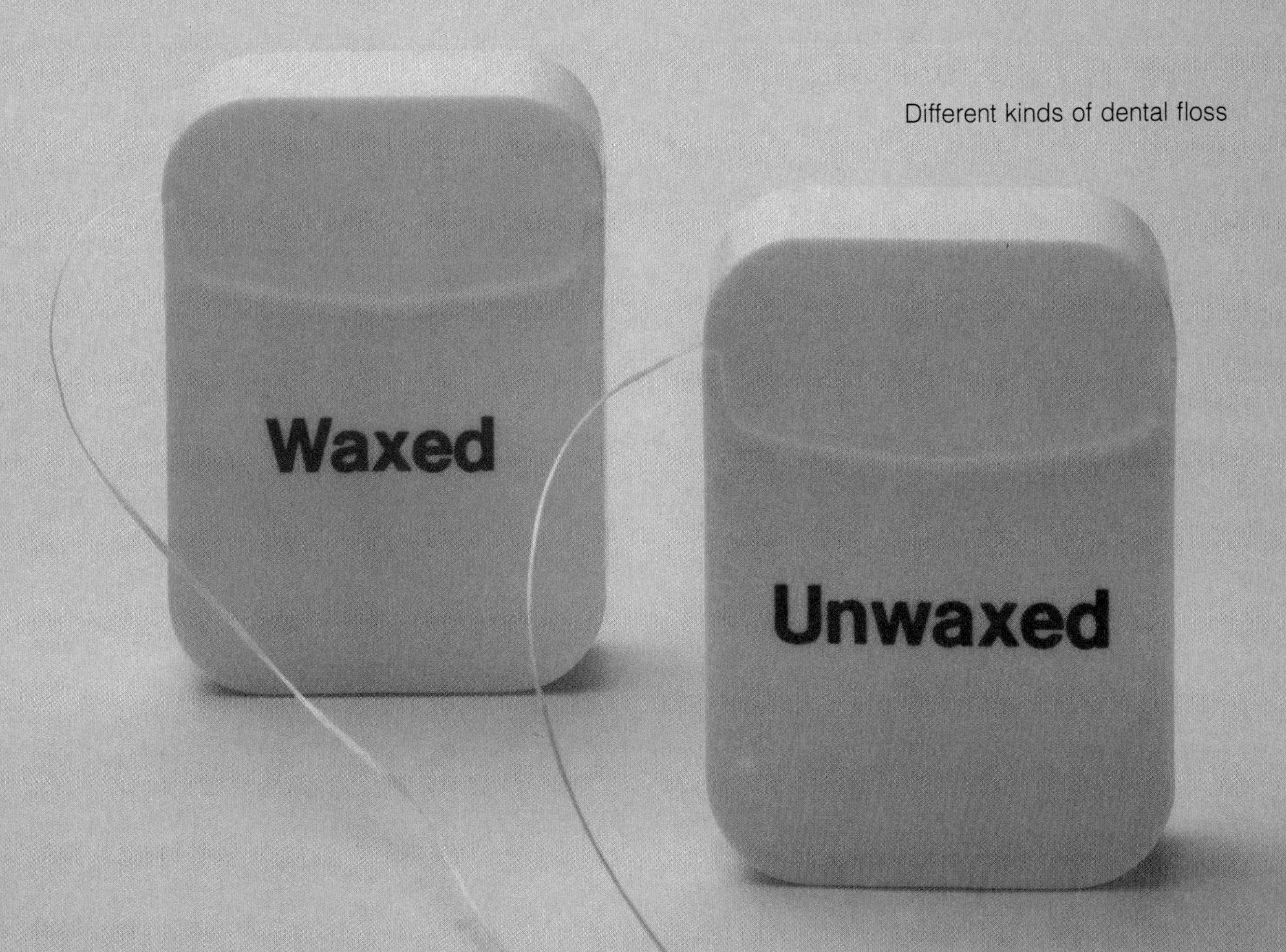

Different kinds of dental floss

William Addis's Toothbrush

Suppose you did not have a toothbrush. What would you use to clean your teeth?

Many hundreds of years ago, people did not have toothbrushes. Some people cleaned their teeth by rubbing them with chalk and a rag. Others cleaned their teeth by scraping them with a twig about the size of a pencil. People first soaked the twig in water. Then they pounded the twig on one end until the end looked like a brush.

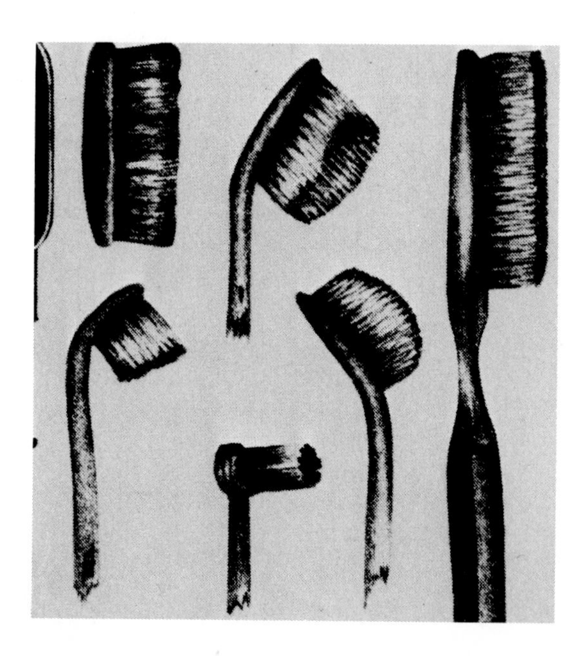

Many people began using toothbrushes about two hundred years ago because of William Addis. In 1780 he started a company to make toothbrushes. William Addis used ox bones to make the backs and handles of his toothbrushes. The bones were boiled to remove fat and grease. Then the bones were cut in the shape of a toothbrush. Small holes were drilled in the bones. The holes were stuffed with bristles made of white horsetail hair. The picture shows some toothbrushes like the ones William Addis made.

The company that William Addis started is still making toothbrushes. The toothbrushes are no longer made from bone and horsetail hair. Now the handles are made from plastic and the bristles from nylon.

Talk About It

1. How did William Addis make toothbrushes?
2. If you were making a new kind of toothbrush, what would it be like?

Chapter 4 Review

Reviewing Lesson Objectives

1. Tell what the enamel, root, blood vessels, and nerves in a tooth do. (pages 94–96)
2. Tell what jobs the primary teeth do. (pages 98–101)
3. Tell how plaque can harm teeth and gums. (pages 102–103)
4. Tell how brushing and flossing, eating healthy foods, and visiting a dentist help keep teeth and gums healthy. (pages 104–109)
5. Tell who can help advise people about good products for tooth care. (pages 112–115)

For further review, use Study Guide pages 228–229.

Checking Health Vocabulary

Number your paper from 1–8. Match each meaning in Column I with the correct word or words in Column II.

Column I

1. the part of the tooth above the gum
2. the hard outer covering that protects a tooth
3. the first twenty teeth that come through the gums
4. the second set of teeth
5. a sticky material made up of germs
6. a hole in a tooth caused by acid
7. strong thread that can help clean between the teeth
8. a person who uses special tools to clean teeth and also takes X rays of teeth

Column II

a. cavity
b. crown
c. dental floss
d. dental hygienist
e. enamel
f. permanent teeth
g. plaque
h. primary teeth

Chapter 4 Test

Complete the Sentence

Number your paper from 1–9. Next to each number write the word that best completes the sentence. Choose the words from the list below.

between	plaque
cavities	primary
dentists	size
nerves	teeth
permanent	

1. The ____ in the center of a tooth send messages from the tooth to the brain.
2. The ____ teeth hold space open so a second set of teeth can come in straight.
3. If a person takes care of his or her ____ teeth, they can last a lifetime.
4. Plaque is always forming on ____ and between them.
5. Teeth and gums can be harmed by ____.
6. Brushing and flossing teeth can help prevent ____.
7. Dental floss is used to clean ____ teeth.
8. People who can give the best advice about tooth care are ____ or dental hygienists.
9. A person should use a toothbrush that is the right ____ for his or her mouth.

Short Answer

Number your paper from 10–18. Next to each number write the word or words that best answer the question.

10. What carries nutrients and oxygen to a tooth?
11. What helps hold the tooth in the jawbone?
12. Where are teeth that grind food found in the mouth?
13. How long should permanent teeth last?
14. What can plaque built up where the teeth and gums meet cause?
15. What can flossing remove from between the teeth?
16. How does eating foods from the four food groups help teeth and gums?
17. What does a dentist use to clean teeth?
18. What do toothpastes with the ADA seal help prevent?

Essay

Write the answers on your paper. Use complete sentences.

19. What advice would you give about buying a toothbrush?
20. What could help you remember to brush your teeth daily?

Health at Home

Caring for Your Teeth at Home

Talk with your family about ways to help keep the teeth and gums healthy. What can you tell your family about brushing and flossing the teeth?

Maybe you can draw a picture to show your family. Make a drawing that shows something you have learned about caring for the teeth. What does this girl's picture show?

Reading at Home

Michael and the Dentist by Bernard Wolf. Four Winds Press, 1980. Find out what happens when Michael visits the dentist.

Teeth by John Gaskin. Franklin Watts Inc., 1984. Learn about the different kinds of teeth and how to take care of your teeth.

Chapter 5

You and Your Safety

What are these children doing to help keep themselves safe? How can you help keep yourself safe?

The lessons in this chapter will help you learn many ways to keep safe throughout your life.

1. Who Is Most Responsible for Keeping You Safe?
2. How Can You Keep Safe in a Car?
3. How Can You Keep Safe on a Bicycle?
4. How Can You Keep Safe with Electric Appliances?
5. How Can You Keep Safe with Products Around the House?
6. How Can You Keep Safe While Swimming?
7. How Can You Act Safely to Prevent Injuries From Fires?
8. How Can You Help If an Injury Happens?

S1700

1 Who Is Most Responsible for Keeping You Safe?

Suppose you were waiting to cross the street as this girl is doing. What would you do before crossing? What is the safe way to be sure you cross after all cars have stopped?

The girl knows that she is responsible for keeping herself safe. She is following a safety rule that she has learned. She always waits on the curb and looks left, right, and then left again before crossing any street. Following this rule helps keep her safe.

Just like this girl, you are responsible for keeping yourself safe. Other people can only help keep you safe. You are most responsible for your own safety. Following safety rules can help keep you safe.

This girl looks to the left, right, and then left again to keep herself safe.

Being careful can help keep you safe. For example, you can help prevent an **injury** when you watch where you walk on stairs. You do not want to fall and hurt yourself. Hold on to a railing if possible.

Thinking of ways to prevent accidents can also help keep you safe. Suppose you and your friends want to play ball in the park. Before you play, you should carefully check the playing field for sharp objects. How might this rule help prevent injuries?

injury (in′jər ē), damage to the body.

Think back • *Study on your own with Study Guide page 230.*

1. Who is most responsible for your safety?
2. What can help a person be a safe walker?
3. What can a person do to help prevent accidents?

2 How Can You Keep Safe in a Car?

Suppose you ride in a car that pulls up to the curb. What is the safest way to get out of the car?

You should get in and out of a car on the curb side, as the picture shows. This safety rule helps protect you from other cars in the street.

What safety rules should you follow to help keep you safe in a car? One rule is to lock the doors. Usually a locked door will not open even if someone moves the handle. Locked car doors prevent people from falling out of a car accidentally.

This girl gets out of a car on the curb side to stay safe.

The picture shows the most important rule to follow every time you ride in a car. This rule is to wear your safety belt. You will not be thrown out of your seat if the car stops suddenly.

Another safety rule is to not bother the car driver. How might not bothering the driver help prevent accidents?

Think Back • *Study on your own with Study Guide page 230.*

1. What is the safe way to get in and out of a car?
2. What is the most important safety rule to follow when riding in a car?
3. What are some other safety rules to follow when riding in a car?

On Your Own

You know some safety rules to follow when you are in a car. Which rules can also help keep you safe in a school bus or another bus? Use your own paper, and list other safety rules you can follow in a bus. You might write how the rules can help keep you safe in a bus.

This boy buckles his safety belt when he rides in a car.

3 How Can You Keep Safe on a Bicycle?

Before you drive your bicycle, check to see if it is safe to drive. Ask an adult to help you. The chart tells you what parts to check.

What can help keep you safe while driving your bicycle? Following these safety rules can help keep you safe.

- Drive a bicycle that is the right size for you.
- Learn how to drive your bicycle well.

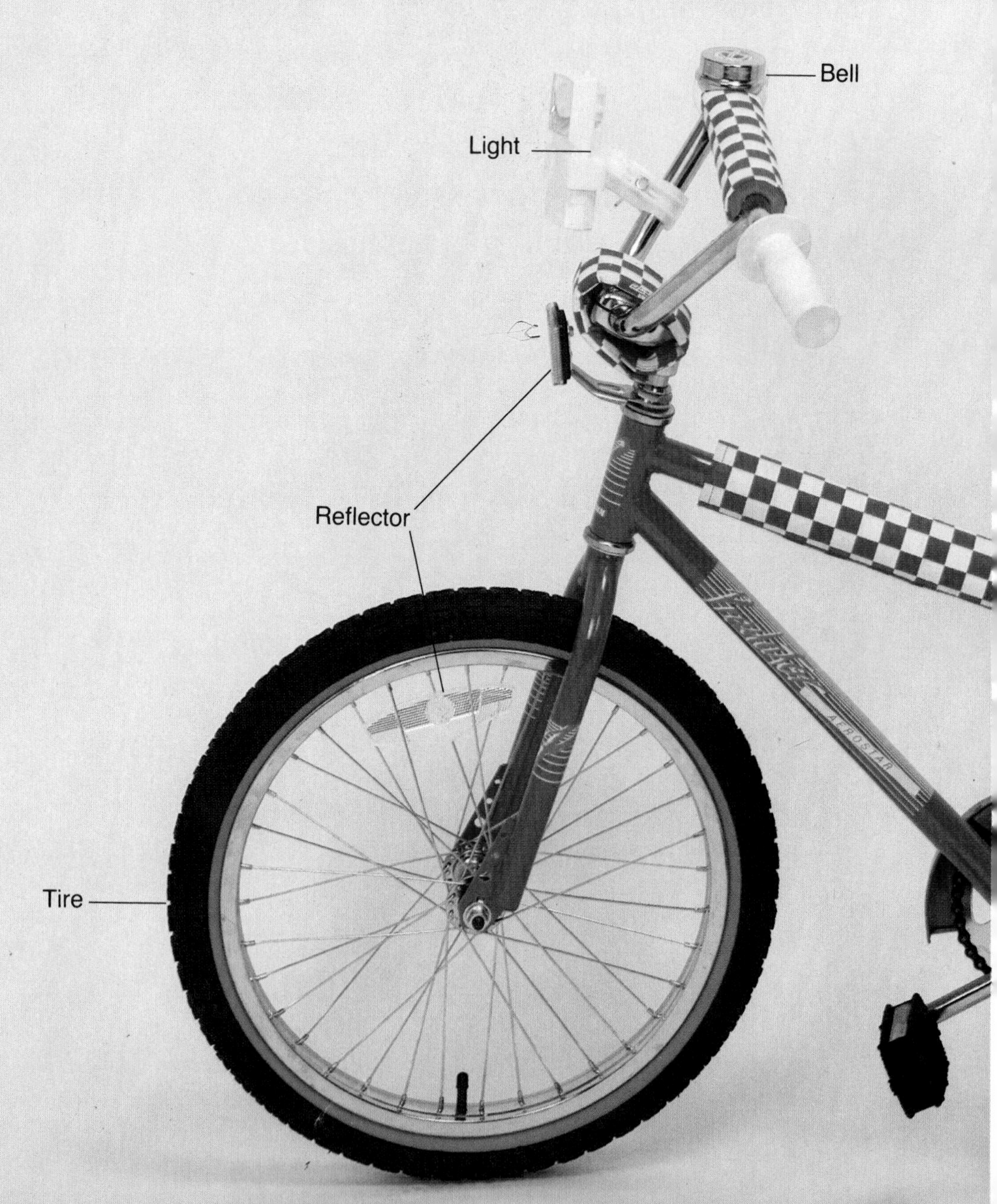

• Learn and use the hand signals for a left turn and a right turn.
• Ride on the sidewalk if your community allows you to.
• Drive on the right-hand side of the sidewalk or street.
• Drive in single file if you are with other bicycle drivers.

Think Back • *Study on your own with Study Guide page 230.*

1. What parts of a bicycle should be checked before driving?
2. What are some safety rules a bicycle driver should follow?

Bicycle Parts to Check

Check the brakes. Be sure they can stop the bike safely.

Check the tires. Be sure they have enough air in them.

Check to see if your bike has a horn or bell, a light, a chain guard, and reflectors.

electric shock, an injury caused by electricity moving through the body.

4 How Can You Keep Safe with Electric Appliances?

Suppose you are making toast. The toast gets stuck in the toaster. How can you safely remove the stuck toast? Unplug the toaster. The picture shows how you should pull the plug. Never pull on the cord. Ask an adult in your family to help you remove the toast. Then you will not burn yourself.

A toaster is an electric appliance. It uses electricity to do a job. Electricity can be helpful, but it can also be harmful. It can cause fires. Electricity can also cause injuries such as burns and **electric shocks.** Handle an electric appliance carefully to stay safe.

Pull on the plug to safely unplug an electric appliance. Never pull on the cord.

Never touch small electric appliances with wet hands. Also, never touch small electric appliances when you are standing or sitting in water. Electricity can travel through the water and give you a shock.

When you finish using a small appliance that heats up, turn it off. Then unplug the appliance. Sparks might come out of the socket if the appliance is not turned off. The sparks can cause a fire. You could get burned.

Think Back • *Study on your own with Study Guide page 230.*

1. What is the safe way to unplug an electric appliance?
2. What are some safe ways to handle electric appliances?

Dry your hands before touching an electric appliance.

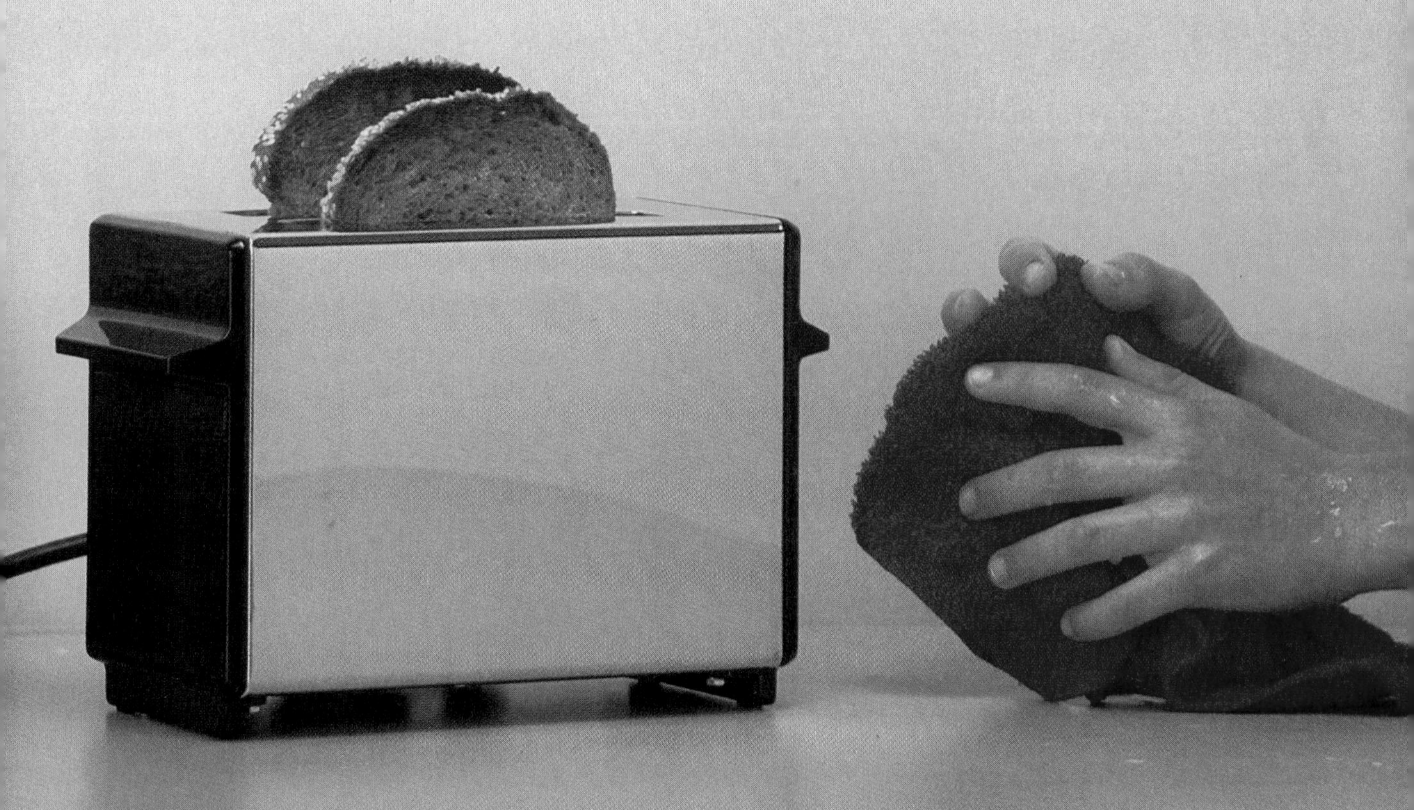

poison (poi′zn), a substance that if taken into or put on the body can be dangerous to life or health.

5 How Can You Keep Safe with Products Around the House?

People must be very careful when using certain products in their homes. The picture shows some of these products. People use many of these products for cleaning and repairing the home. Which of these products have you seen? The products contain **poisons** that can be harmful.

Many products need to be used only in rooms with lots of fresh air. People can be safe using products that might be harmful by following these safety rules.

- Leave the labels on the products so that people can easily read any warnings.

These products should be used and stored carefully. They contain poisons.

• Read the directions on the label of a product before using it. Be sure to open a window if the directions say to do so.
• Keep all the products in the containers they come in. Do not put them in different containers.
• Do not mix different cleaning products together.
• Store all the products away from food. Also, store them out of the reach of small children.

Did You Know?
Some plants, such as Lily-of-the-Valley, have poisonous parts. The parts can harm anyone who eats them. Always place plants out of the reach of small children in the home.

Think Back • *Study on your own with Study Guide page 231.*

1. Why must people be careful when using certain products around the house?
2. What are some safety rules to follow when using products that contain poisons?

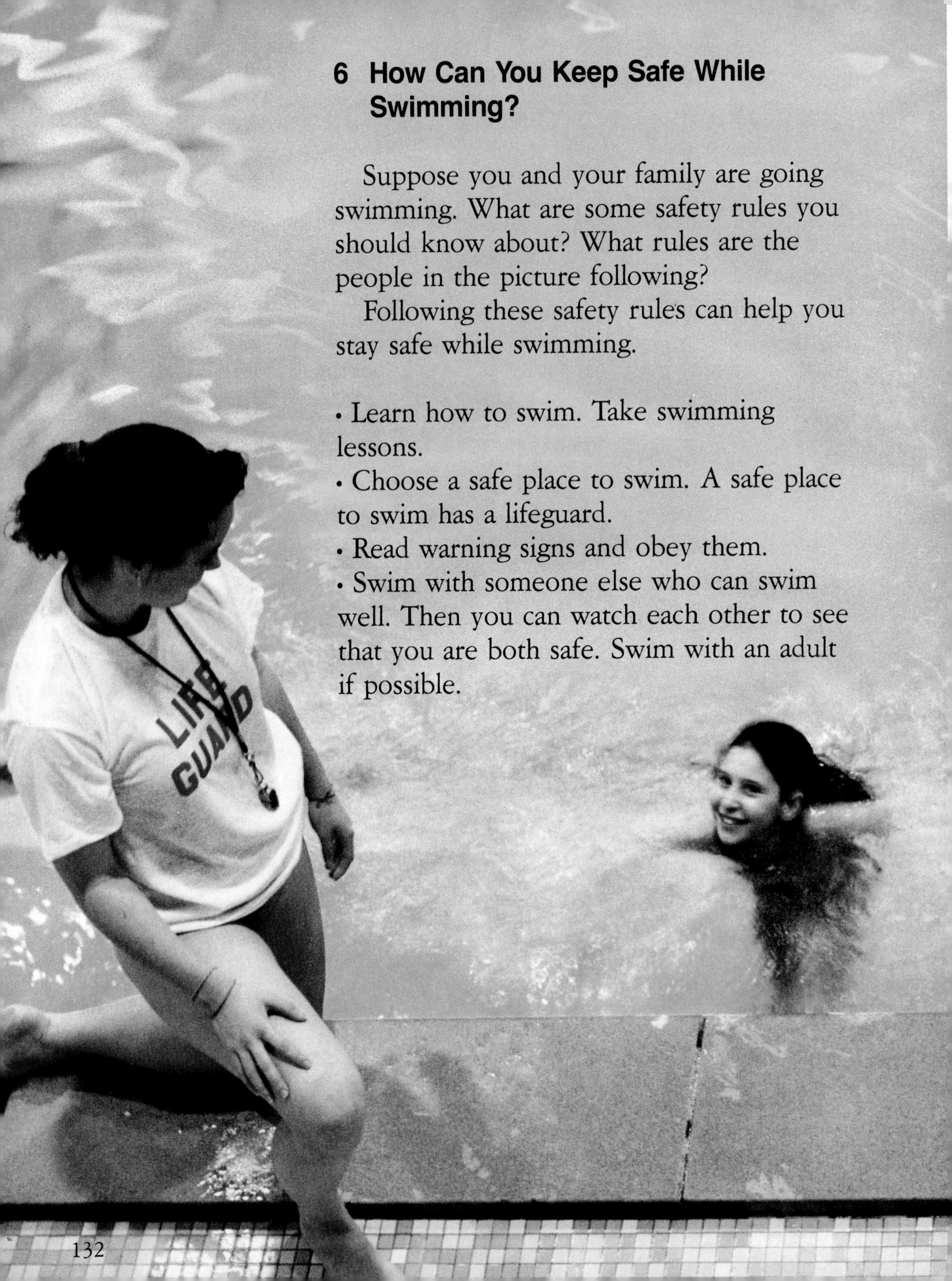

6 How Can You Keep Safe While Swimming?

Suppose you and your family are going swimming. What are some safety rules you should know about? What rules are the people in the picture following?

Following these safety rules can help you stay safe while swimming.

- Learn how to swim. Take swimming lessons.
- Choose a safe place to swim. A safe place to swim has a lifeguard.
- Read warning signs and obey them.
- Swim with someone else who can swim well. Then you can watch each other to see that you are both safe. Swim with an adult if possible.

• Call for help if you need it. Never call for help as a joke.
• Stay out of deep water unless you are a good swimmer.
• Swim only when you feel well. Come out of the water if you feel tired or cold.
• Be careful when you are around water. Do not push or run.

How can following these safety rules help keep you safe?

Think Back • *Study on your own with Study Guide page 231.*

1. What are some safety rules to follow before going swimming?
2. What are some safety rules to follow when swimming?

These swimmers want to swim safely. What ways can they stay safe?

Health Activities Workshop

Keeping Safe

1. Solve this puzzle on a sheet of paper. Find out what to do if you are swimming and you see lightning.

C_m_ __t _f th_ w_t_r.

L_ghtn_ng m_ght str_k_ th_ w_t_r.

Th_n _l_ctr_c_ty c__ld tr_v_l thr__gh th_ w_t_r.

_t c__ld tr_v_l t_ y__ _nd g_v_ y__ a sh_ck.

2. Explain how following the safety rule shown can help save lives. Draw yourself following another safety rule in a car.

3. Make up a play about the safety rules you should follow while driving a bicycle. Pretend you are talking to young children. What will you tell them?

Looking at Careers

4. You might like to become a **firefighter** if you think you would enjoy helping keep people safe. A firefighter works to prevent fires. One way a firefighter prevents fires is to make a safety check of a building. Another way is to visit schools and tell about ways to prevent fires. If a fire does happen, a firefighter works to put out the fire. A firefighter also works to save people's lives and homes.

You might want to find a book in the library about firefighters. Find out what a firefighter wears for protection when fighting a fire.

7 How Can You Act Safely to Prevent Injuries from Fires?

What does this family put in their home to help prevent injuries from fires?

Putting one or more smoke alarms in your home can help you if a fire starts. An alarm makes a loud sound when smoke reaches it. An alarm can warn you in time for you to escape a fire without injury. You should leave your home as quickly as possible if a smoke alarm sounds.

Smoke alarms help people stay safe by warning of fires.

Sometimes people are injured when their clothes catch on fire. Stop where you are if your clothes catch on fire. Put your hands over your face to help protect it from flames. Drop down and roll on the floor. Roll to put out the fire and help prevent injuries. The boy in the picture is practicing dropping to the floor and rolling. Practicing helps him remember what to do if his clothes ever catch on fire.

Why should you stop, drop, and roll? You will smother the fire that way. Never run if your clothes catch on fire. Running makes the flames burn more.

Did You Know?
During fires, more people are injured by breathing smoke and gases than by being burned.

Stop, drop, and roll to smother a fire.

What Should You Do in Case of a Fire?

Suppose you are in your bedroom when you hear a smoke alarm sound. Leave the bedroom door closed if it feels hot. A hot door means fire is on the other side. Try to get out of the room another way. Leave by a window if possible. Wait on a porch or roof for the fire department.

If you cannot get out of the room, stuff clothes or bedding under the door. This helps keep out smoke and dangerous gases. Then open a window and stay near it. Hold a cloth over your nose and mouth as this girl is doing. The cloth helps keep you from breathing in smoke and gases. Wait for firefighters to come for you.

Suppose the bedroom door feels cool. Then, open the door slowly and crawl out.

Wait near an open window for firefighters if you cannot get out of a room.

Crawling, as shown, helps prevent injuries caused by breathing in smoke and dangerous gases. Smoke and gases rise upward. You will not breathe in much smoke or gases if you crawl along the floor.

Do not go back into your home for any reason once you get out. Call the fire department from a neighbor's home. Look around for family members. They will want to know that you are safe.

On Your Own
Suppose you are looking out your window. You notice smoke coming out of the building next door. List everything you could do to help. What is the most important thing that you should not do?

Think Back • *Study on your own with Study Guide page 231.*

1. How can a smoke alarm help prevent injuries from fires?
2. What should be done if clothes catch on fire?
3. How can crawling help prevent injuries caused by breathing in smoke and dangerous gases?

This boy is practicing the right way to crawl out of a room during a fire.

8 How Can You Help If an Injury Happens?

You probably try to stay safe when you play. Injuries sometimes happen even when you try to play safely. What should you do if a friend is badly injured while you are playing?

You should follow these rules if someone you are with is injured.

- Stay calm. Try not to get upset. Staying calm helps you think better.
- Try to get adult help. Shout for help. Go for help if no one comes. Tell the injured person where you are going and that you will be back. Try to find a parent or an adult neighbor to help.
- Telephone for help if you cannot find an adult. Some areas have an emergency number that you can call. This number is 911. You can also dial the number 0. An operator will help you if you dial 0. If you have a list of emergency numbers by your telephone, call one of them.
- Speak slowly and clearly when you call to report an injury.
- Listen to any directions that you are given. Follow those directions. Do not hang up the telephone until the person you are talking to hangs up.

The girl shown here is reporting an injury. What is she telling the operator?

This girl is reporting an injury to the operator. She is telling the operator her name, her address, and her telephone number. She is also describing the injury. She will wait to hear what the operator says before she hangs up.

first aid, immediate care given for an injury.

What First Aid Can You Give?

Suppose someone has a small injury such as a small cut. Tell an adult about the injury. How can you help?

You can give **first aid** to others or to yourself for a small injury. First aid is help you give right after an injury.

What first aid can you give for a small cut? First, wash the cut with soap and water. Next, dry the cut with a clean tissue or towel. Then cover the cut with a bandage to help keep the cut clean. Press gently on the bandage if the cut keeps bleeding. The bleeding will soon stop.

Look at the picture. What is the boy doing to help?

The girl's cut has been washed with soap and dried. How will the bandage help the cut?

Sometimes insect bites cause pain, itching, or swelling. Tell an adult about an insect bite that bothers you. The adult can help you if you need first aid.

You should first run cold water over an insect bite to help stop the pain or itching. Then put a cloth with ice on top of the bite. Ice also helps stop pain and swelling. What is the boy in the picture doing for his insect bite?

Think Back • *Study on your own with Study Guide page 231.*

1. How can staying calm help in an emergency?
2. What are some ways to get adult help if someone is injured?
3. What first aid should be given for a small cut?
4. What first aid should be given for an insect bite?

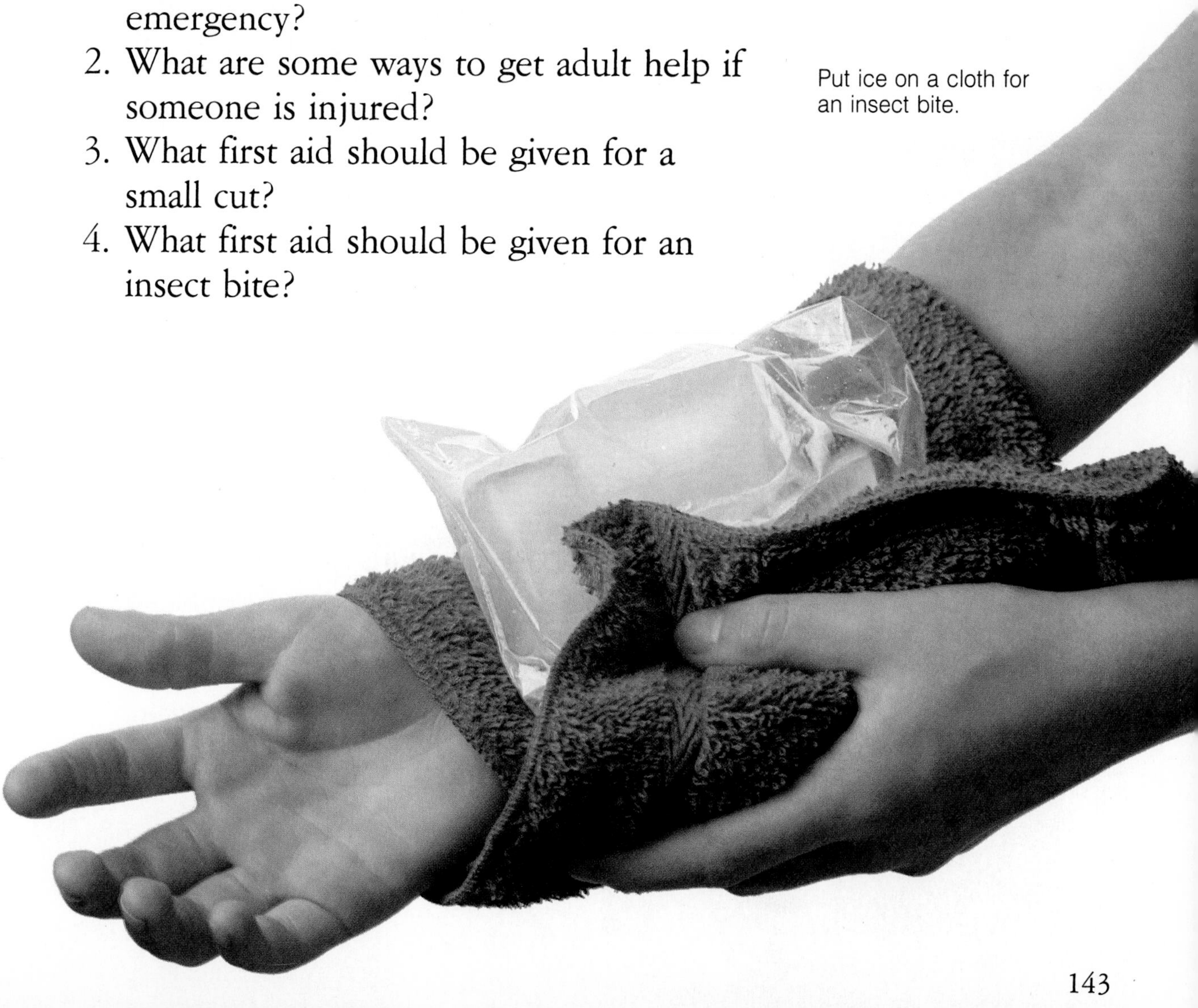

Put ice on a cloth for an insect bite.

Health Focus

Dawnita Reinhardt Works to Help Save Lives

Dawnita Reinhardt always buckles her safety belt when she gets in a car. She knows wearing safety belts helps save lives. She thinks she is alive because she used a safety belt.

Dawnita was in a serious car accident when she was sixteen years old. The police who helped at the accident think that Dawnita could not have lived unless she had her safety belt buckled.

Dawnita Reinhardt now works to help save people's lives. She tells people about the importance of using safety belts. Dawnita gives talks at club meetings about using safety belts. She made a television advertisement about using safety belts. Dawnita also wrote a safety booklet for children. In the booklet, Example Elephant gives children some reasons for using safety belts.

Talk About It

1. How does Dawnita Reinhardt work to help save car riders' lives?
2. What could you do to help save people's lives?

Chapter 5 Review

Reviewing Lesson Objectives

1. Tell who is most responsible for a person's safety. (pages 122–123)
2. List some safety rules to follow when riding in a car. (pages 124–125)
3. Tell what should be checked on a bicycle to see if it is safe to drive. List some safety rules to follow while driving a bicycle. (pages 126–127)
4. Tell about some safe ways to handle electric appliances. (pages 128–129)
5. List some safety rules to follow when using products that contain or give off poisons. (pages 130–131)
6. List some safety rules to follow when swimming. (pages 132–133)
7. Tell how injuries from fires can be prevented. (pages 136–139)
8. Tell how to get adult help if someone is injured. Tell how to give first aid for small injuries. (pages 140–143)

For further review, use Study Guide pages 230-231.

Checking Health Vocabulary

Number your paper from 1–4. Match each meaning in Column I with the correct word or words in Column II.

Column I

1. damage to the body
2. a substance that if taken into or put on the body can be dangerous to life or health
3. immediate care given for an injury
4. an injury caused by electricity moving through the body

Column II

a. electric shock
b. first aid
c. injury
d. poison

Chapter 5 Test

Complete the Sentence

Number your paper from 1–9. Next to each number write the word that best completes the sentence. Choose the words from the list below.

careful
clearly
crawl
lifeguard
parts
plug
products
protect
safety

1. Being ____ can help keep you safe.
2. To stay safe when riding in a car, wear a ____ belt.
3. To keep safe on a bicycle, check the bicycle ____ and follow safety rules.
4. To safely unplug an electric appliance, pull on its ____.
5. Keep all ____ in the containers they came in.
6. To ____ small children, store cleaning products out of their reach.
7. A safe place to swim has a ____.
8. To help prevent injuries caused by breathing in smoke, ____ out of a room.
9. Speak slowly and ____ when telephoning to report an injury.

Short Answer

Number your paper from 10–16. Next to each number write the word or words that best answer the question.

10. Who is most responsible for a person's safety?
11. What side of a car is safe to get in and out of?
12. Who should help a child give a bicycle a safety check?
13. What should be read before using any product that contains poisons?
14. How can swimming with someone else who swims well help keep a person safe?
15. What three words should a person remember if his or her clothes catch on fire?
16. How can ice or cold water help an insect bite?

Essay

Write the answers on your paper. Use complete sentences.

17. What are two safety rules an adult can follow if someone is injured?
18. What is another way fires in home kitchens can be prevented other than using electric appliances carefully?

Health at Home

Being Safe at Home

Talk with your family about safety. Talk about ways to help keep the family safe at home.

You might want to make a safety check of your home as this family is doing. For example, you might check if small appliances are unplugged when not being used. What safety check might be made with cleaning products around the house? You might talk over ways to make your home as safe as possible.

Reading at Home

Fire! Fire! by Gail Gibbons. T.Y. Crowell, 1984. Learn how firefighters fight fires.

What to Do When Your Mom or Dad Says Be Prepared! by Joy Wilt Berry. Bartholomew, 1982. Learn how to prepare for an emergency.

Chapter 6

Medicines, Drugs, and Your Health

What is this person handling? If you answered medicines, you are correct. She knows a lot about medicines. For example, she knows how different kinds of medicines can help people.

You need to know about medicines too. You need to know safe ways to use medicines. Some medicines can be harmful if not used correctly.

The lessons in this chapter tell how to use medicines safely. Learning how and when to use medicines can help keep you healthy throughout your life.

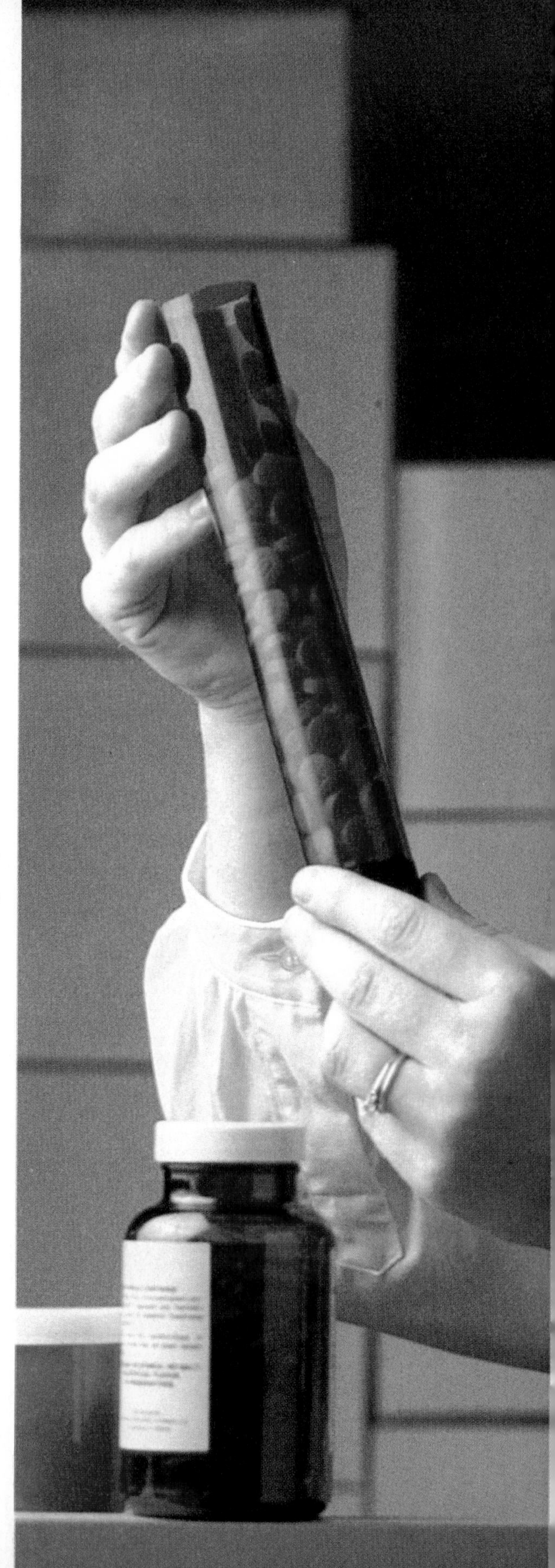

prescription (pri skrip′shən) **medicine,** a medicine that can be bought only with a doctor's order.

On Your Own
Write a story telling how the doctor in the picture is helping the parent and child.

1 What Are Different Kinds of Medicines?

Medicines can help people get well or feel better. Medicines also keep people from getting sick.

Medicines are a kind of drug. All drugs cause changes in the body. Drugs can also change how a person thinks, feels, or acts. Because drugs can make these changes, they must be used with care.

A **prescription medicine** is a medicine that people need a doctor's order to buy. The order is called a prescription. It tells the name of the person who will use the medicine. It also tells how much medicine should be used and how often. What is this doctor writing?

People usually get a prescription medicine at a drugstore. A pharmacist fills the order for a prescription medicine. He or she puts a label on the medicine. The name of the medicine and directions for use are on the label. The name of the person who will use the medicine is also on the label. The prescription medicine is for one person only.

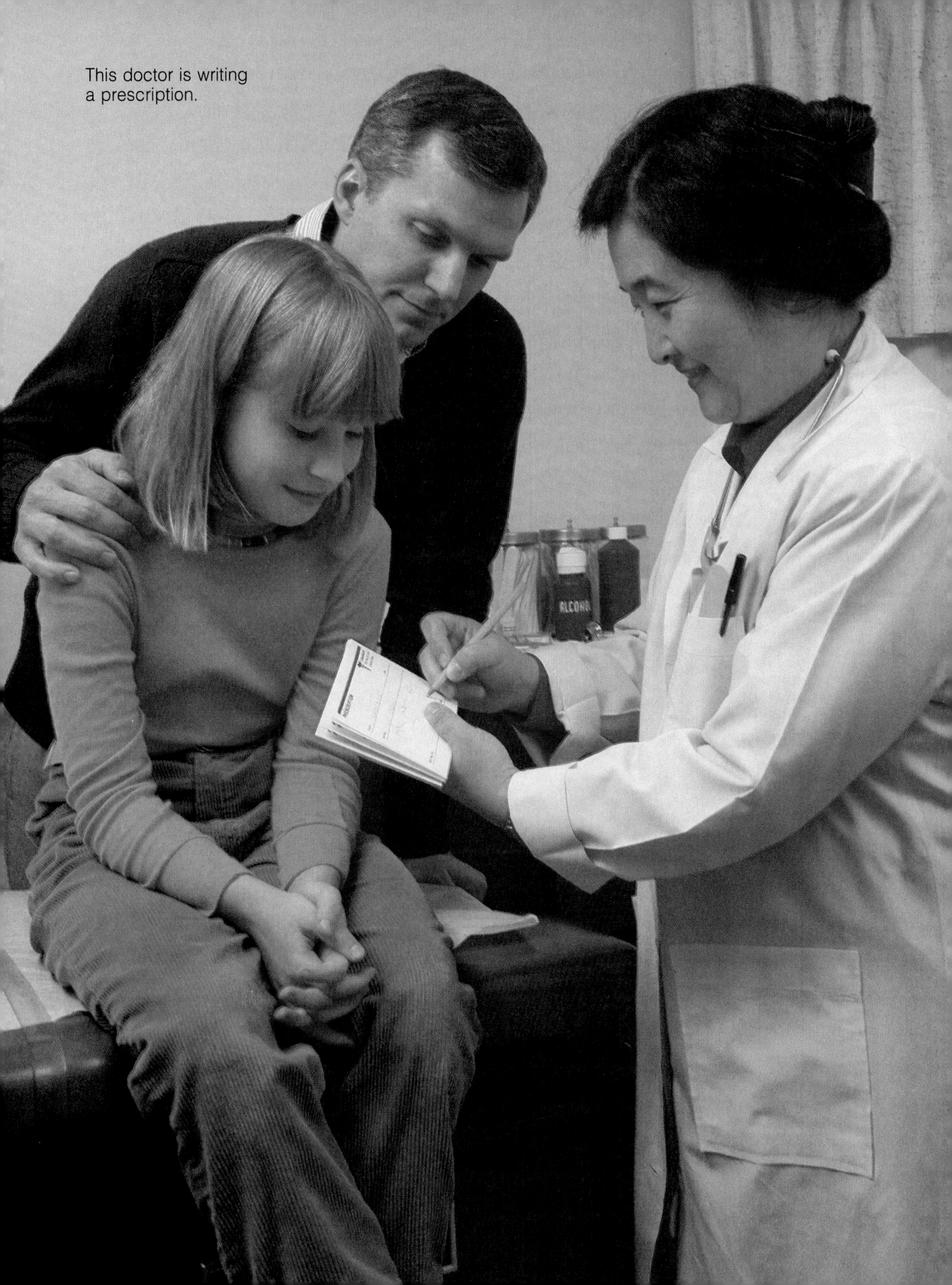

This doctor is writing a prescription.

over-the-counter medicine, a medicine that can be bought without a prescription.

What Are Over-the-Counter Medicines?

An **over-the-counter medicine** is another kind of medicine that people use. People do not need a prescription to buy this kind of medicine. Cough syrups and medicines for a fever are examples of over-the-counter medicines. The labels and boxes of many over-the-counter medicines have directions for using the medicines. A pharmacist can also give people information about using these medicines.

Drugstores sell over-the-counter medicines. Some supermarkets and department stores also sell them. What over-the-counter medicines do you see here? What other over-the-counter medicines do you know about?

Think Back • *Study on your own with Study Guide page 232.*

1. How can medicines help people?
2. What is a prescription medicine?
3. What is an over-the-counter medicine?

Stores sell many different kinds of over-the-counter medicines.

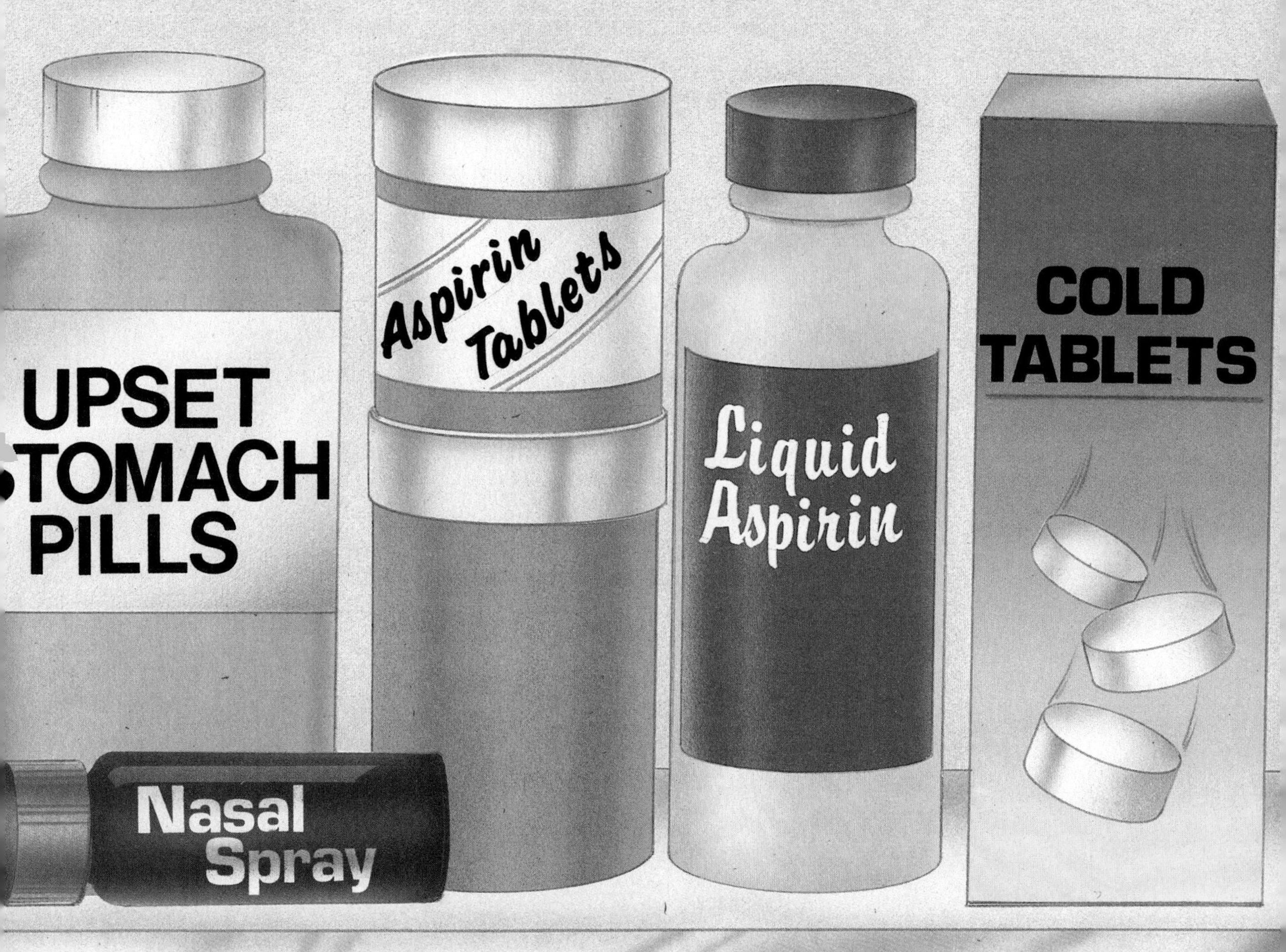

2 Why Do People Use Medicines?

Medicines can help sick people. Some medicines help cure diseases. Some medicines help prevent diseases. Some medicines help sick people feel better.

Some medicines help cure diseases by killing germs that cause the diseases. Germs are tiny things that are too small for you to see. Germs can be everywhere. Air, water, and soil have germs. You have germs inside you and on your skin all the time. Some germs cause diseases, but most germs will not harm you.

Germs must get inside the body to cause diseases. How can germs get inside the body?

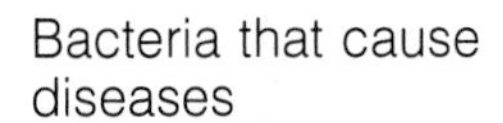

Bacteria that cause diseases

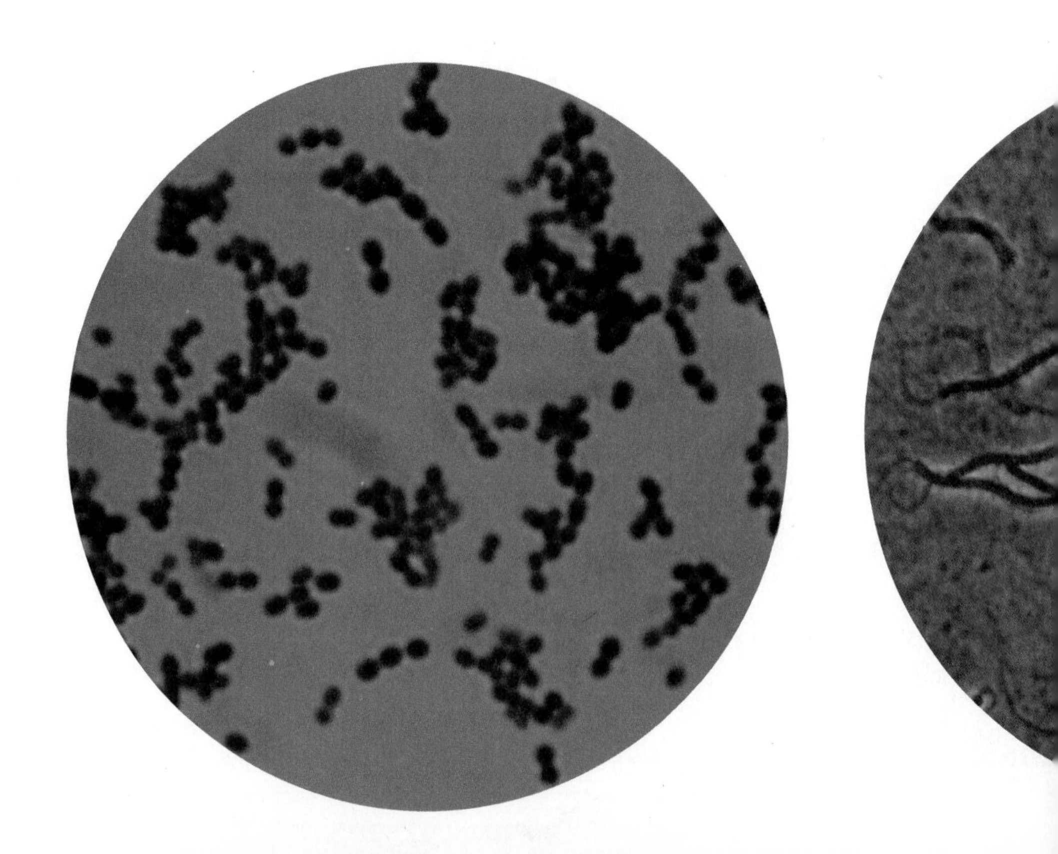

Germs can get into the body when a person breathes. Germs can also get into the body through cuts or scrapes on the skin. Sometimes the germs grow when they get inside the body. They might divide many times to make more germs. If germs upset the way the body works, a person becomes sick.

Different kinds of germs can cause diseases. **Bacteria** are one kind of germ that can cause diseases. For example, bacteria cause strep throat and tuberculosis (tü bėr′kyə lō′sis).

The picture shows some bacteria that can cause diseases. The bacteria are shown much larger than they really are. Some medicines can kill these bacteria and help cure the diseases that the bacteria cause.

bacteria (bak tir′ē ə), certain living things made of one cell that can cause diseases such as strep throat and tuberculosis.

On Your Own
On a sheet of paper, describe the shapes of the bacteria in the picture

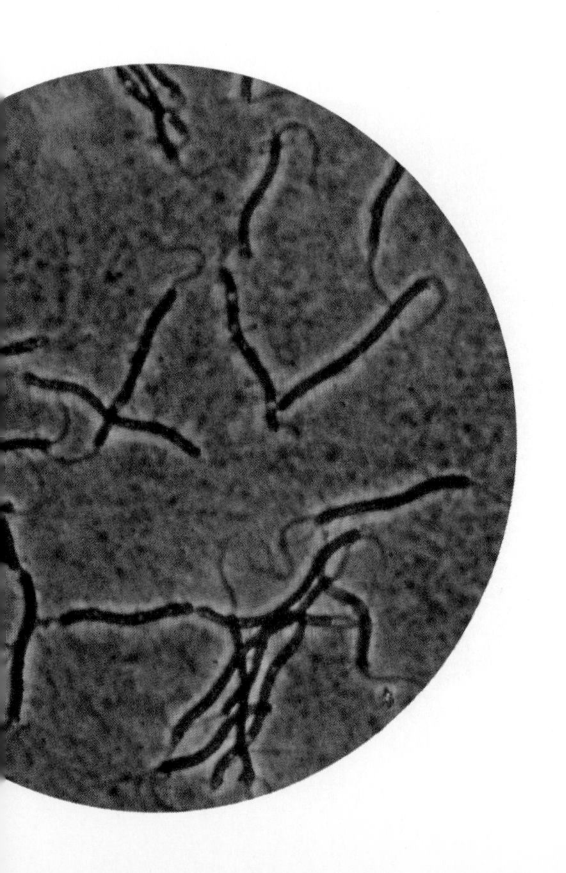

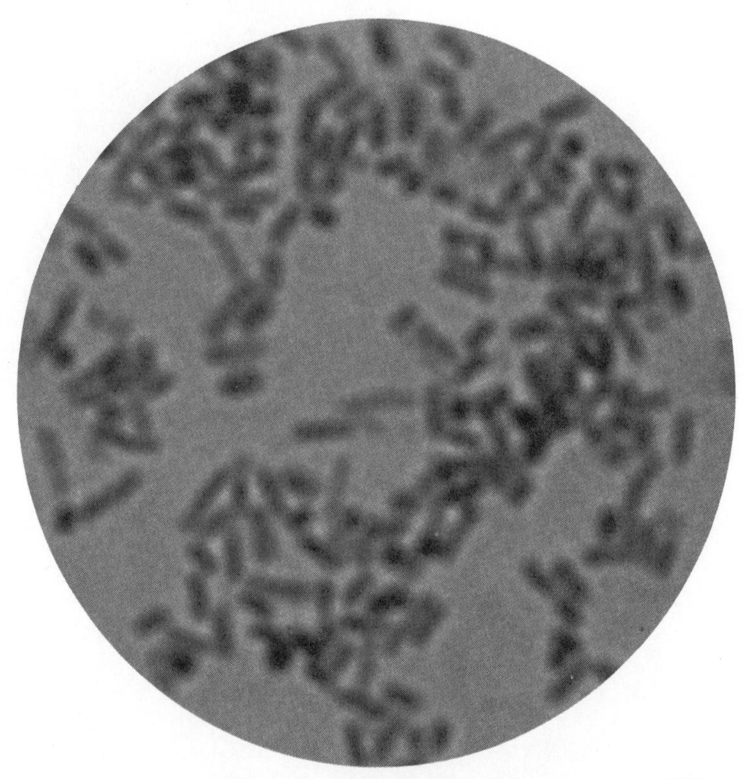

vaccine (vak′sēn′), a medicine that can prevent a disease.

virus (vī′rəs), a tiny germ that can cause diseases such as measles, mumps, and polio.

What Are Vaccines?

Vaccines are medicines that can help prevent diseases. Most people get vaccines in shots.

People get vaccines to prevent diseases such as measles, mumps, and polio. Measles vaccine and mumps vaccine are given as shots. Polio vaccine is given as drops in the mouth.

Germs called **viruses** cause measles, mumps, and polio. Viruses are much smaller than bacteria. What kinds of viruses are shown in the picture?

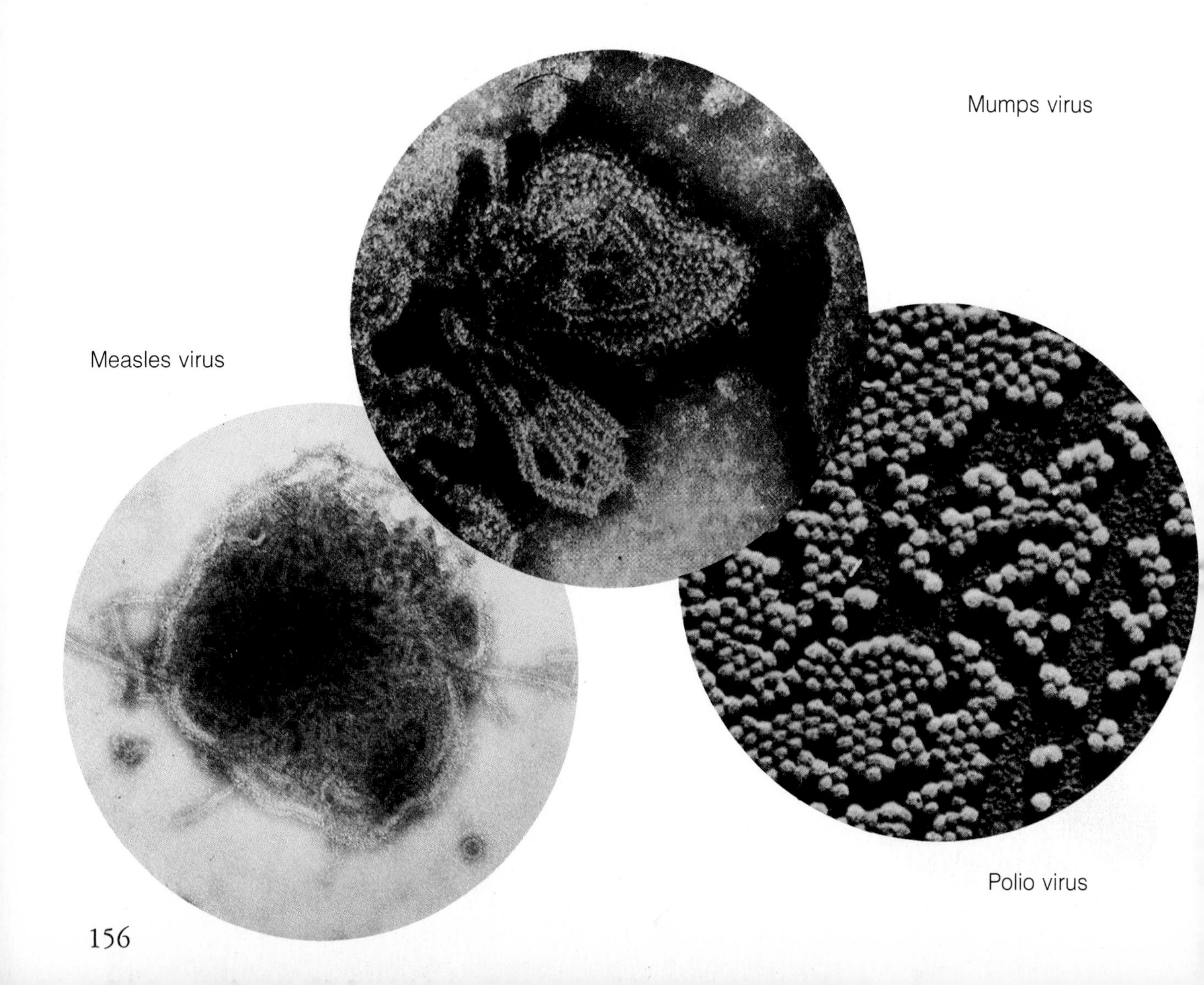

Mumps virus

Measles virus

Polio virus

How Do Medicines Help People Feel Better?

The girl shown here has a broken arm. Her arm hurt badly at first. Her doctor gave her medicine. Now she feels better.

The medicine did not help heal the broken bone. The medicine helped lessen the pain in her arm. Some medicines can help people feel better by taking away pain.

Did You Know?
Some medicines are placed on the skin. Then the medicines pass through the skin into the body. One such medicine helps prevent people from getting sick while traveling in a car. The medicine is in a special patch that is placed on the skin behind an ear.

Think Back • *Study on your own with Study Guide page 232.*

1. What ways are medicines used?
2. What kinds of germs cause diseases?
3. How do germs cause a person to become sick?

Sometimes medicines can help a person feel better. Medicine helped take away the pain in this girl's arm.

side effect, an unwanted change caused by taking a medicine.

Did You Know?
Many over-the-counter medicines now have sealed packages. These packages help keep people who buy the medicines safe. If a sealed medicine package is broken open, people should not buy or use the medicine.

3 How Can People Be Safe with Medicines?

Medicines can harm people if used in the wrong way. People should follow these rules for safety with medicines.

- Only an adult in charge of a child should give the child medicine. The adult should carefully follow the directions on the medicine as this parent is doing.
- Prescription medicines should never be shared. One person's medicine might make another person sick.
- A child should tell an adult in charge about any **side effects** from a medicine. An upset stomach or a headache could be a side effect of a medicine.
- Store medicines in high cabinets, with locks if possible. Then small children cannot reach the medicines or take them.
- Leave the labels on all medicines. People can read the labels to be sure they take the right medicine.
- Keep medicine containers closed. Some medicines have safety caps. Small children cannot open these medicines.

Think Back • *Study on your own with Study Guide page 233.*

1. Who can safely give children medicine?
2. Why should prescription medicine never be shared?
3. How should medicines be stored?

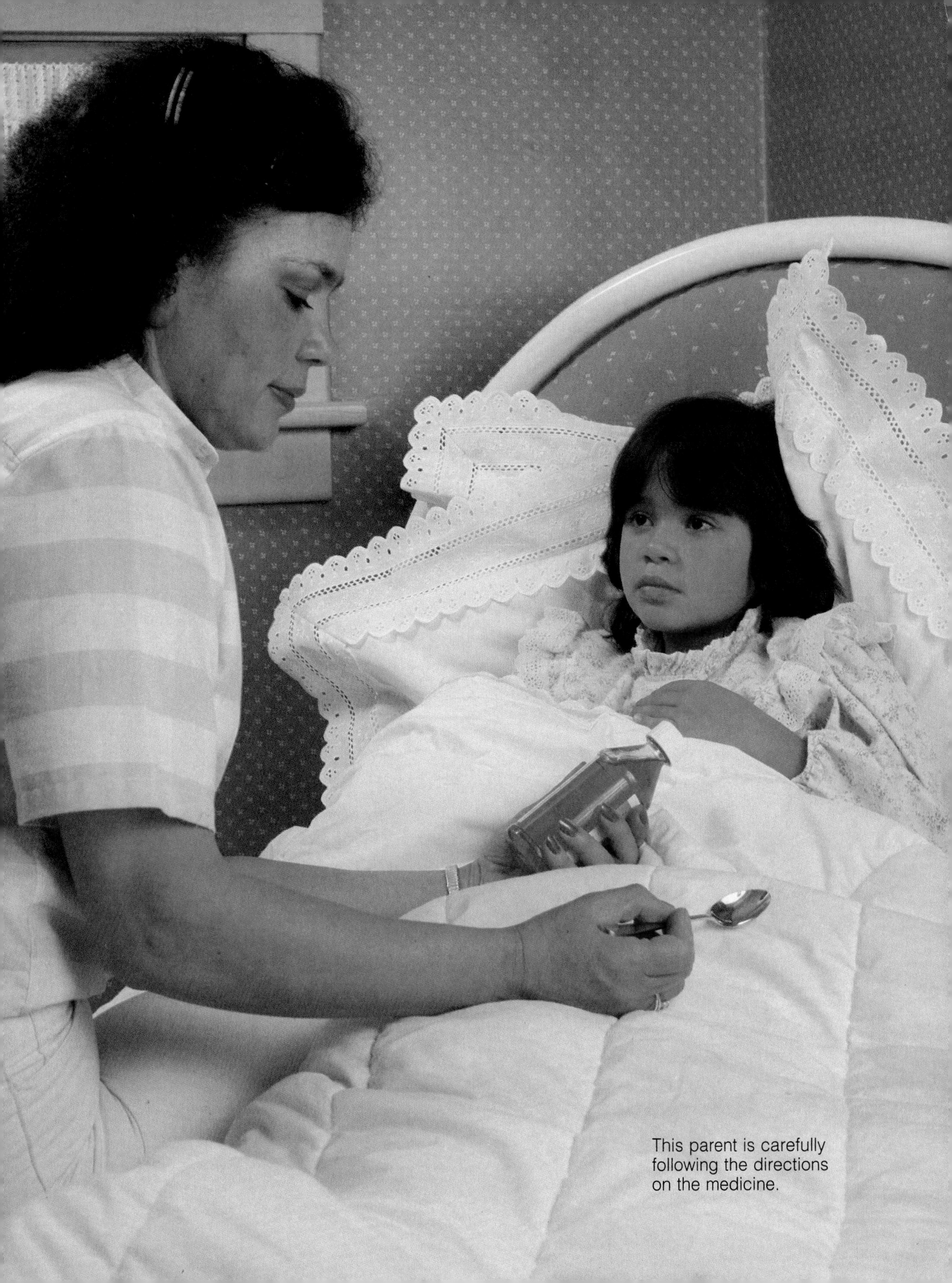

This parent is carefully following the directions on the medicine.

4 What Can You Do Besides Using Medicines?

When have you seen such advertisements for over-the-counter medicines? The ads usually tell how medicines can help you feel better.

Do you always need medicine to help you feel better? Suppose you have a mild headache. Maybe your head aches a little because you need sleep or food. Sleeping or eating might help you feel better. Often tiny aches and pains soon go away. You do not need medicine for every ache or pain.

This advertisement tells you what this medicine can supposedly do.

Sometimes you might not feel well because your feelings are upset. These feelings might make your stomach hurt. Relaxing might help you feel better. The pictures show some ways to relax. Which of these ways would you use to relax?

People should use medicines only if they really need them. Tell an adult in charge of you if you feel sick. The adult or doctor will decide if you need a medicine to feel better.

On Your Own
Look at the pictures of the ways to relax. Write a story about one of the pictures. Write how a person who has upset feelings might use that way of relaxing to feel better.

Think Back • *Study on your own with Study Guide page 233.*

1. What besides medicine can sometimes help a tiny ache or pain go away?
2. When should a person use medicines?

These ways of relaxing can sometimes help a person who is not very sick feel better.

More About Using Medicines

1. A good way to relax is to breathe in deeply. Hold in the breath and count in your mind to five. Then slowly let out the air. Do this several times.

Find out about some other good ways to relax. You might ask your teacher. You might also ask a parent or an adult in charge of you.

2. The poster shows one way to use medicines safely. Think of other ways to use medicines safely. Make a poster about one of these ways. Hang up your poster to remind people to use medicines safely.

Looking at Careers

3. You might see a **pharmacy assistant** helping a pharmacist in a drugstore. The assistant checks to see if the right person's name is on a prescription medicine. He or she also records the name and number of all prescription medicines.

Many pharmacy assistants learn about their jobs while they work in drugstores. Others learn about their jobs by taking special college classes.

Do you think you might enjoy working as a pharmacy assistant? You might like to talk to a pharmacy assistant at a drugstore. Ask the assistant what he or she likes about the job.

caffeine (kaf′ēn′), a drug found in drinks such as coffee, tea, cola, and cocoa. Too much caffeine might harm the body.

These children are enjoying their healthy drinks.

5 What Are Some Harmful Drugs?

Imagine that you have just finished playing a game with your friends. You feel hot and thirsty. You would like a cool drink. The picture shows some healthy drinks. Which drink would you choose?

Some drinks are not healthy. They contain certain drugs. **Caffeine** is a drug found in several drinks. Caffeine can be harmful. Coffee, tea, cola, and cocoa are drinks with caffeine.

Caffeine speeds up the heartbeat. Too much caffeine makes some people feel nervous or causes some people to lose sleep. Doctors think drinks with caffeine in them are not good for young people.

How Is Alcohol Harmful?

Some drinks contain **alcohol.** This drug is found in drinks such as beer, wine, and liquor. Alcohol can be harmful.

Alcohol in drinks goes to the brain very fast. Alcohol changes the way a person's brain works. A person who drinks too much alcohol can have trouble thinking. The person also can have trouble talking clearly, walking, or driving safely.

Suppose a person drinks too much alcohol. What might happen if he or she tries to drive safely?

Alcohol can harm a person's health. A person who often drinks large amounts of alcohol can damage his or her body.

alcohol (al′kə hôl), a drug that can be harmful and is found in beer, wine, and liquor.

nicotine (nik′ə tēn′), a drug in tobacco that can harm a smoker's heart.

Did You Know?
Marijuana cigarettes are more harmful to health than cigarettes made from tobacco. Smoking one marijuana cigarette can cause as much lung damage as smoking twenty-five to thirty tobacco cigarettes.

What Is a Harmful Drug in Cigarettes?

Suppose someone asks a person your age to try smoking a cigarette. What should the person do? A wise person will not ever start smoking.

Cigarettes, cigars, and pipe tobacco have a drug in them called **nicotine.** This drug makes it hard for a smoker to stop smoking. The best idea is not to start smoking.

Nicotine can be a harmful drug. It can cause heart disease in smokers. Nicotine makes the blood vessels smaller. The heart must work very hard to pump blood through the smaller vessels. A person can get heart diseases if his or her heart works too hard.

Cigarette smoke can be harmful too. The smoke contains tars and dangerous gases. Tar is a dark, sticky substance. Tar can build up in the lungs of people who smoke for many years and cause lung cancer.

All cigarette packages have a health warning. What does this warning say?

Why Do People Decide Not to Use Harmful Drugs?

Many people decide not to use any harmful drugs. They know that such drugs can harm their bodies. They also know how hard it is to stop using certain harmful drugs.

These children do not use harmful drugs. These children enjoy playing together. They do not use drugs to feel part of a group. They want to stay healthy.

Think Back • *Study on your own with Study Guide page 233.*

1. How can caffeine harm the body?
2. How can alcohol harm the body?
3. How can nicotine harm the body?
4. What makes people decide not to use harmful drugs?

These children want to stay healthy so they do not use drugs to feel part of a group.

Dr. Percy Julian and Glaucoma Medicine

Dr. Percy Julian was a scientist. During his lifetime, he discovered how to make many medicines. One of these medicines was for the disease glaucoma (glô kō′mə).

A person with glaucoma has too much pressure inside the eyeball. The extra pressure can injure the eyes.

Eyeglasses cannot help a person with glaucoma. Medicines must be used.

The first glaucoma medicines came from plants. Scientists could not get enough of the medicine from plants for all the people with glaucoma. Then Dr. Julian discovered a way to make medicine for glaucoma. He made enough medicine to help many people. Because of Dr. Julian and the medicines later made by other people, those with glaucoma have the helpful medicines they need.

Talk About It

1. What can help people with glaucoma?
2. How might people's lives be different if Dr. Julian had not discovered a way to make medicine for glaucoma?

Chapter 6 Review

Reviewing Lesson Objectives

1. Explain the difference between a prescription medicine and an over-the-counter medicine. (pages 150–153)
2. Tell the uses of medicines and tell what causes some diseases. (pages 154–157)
3. Tell how medicines can be used and stored safely. (pages 158–159)
4. Tell what sometimes can be done to feel better without use of medicines. (pages 160–161)
5. Tell how caffeine, alcohol, and nicotine can harm the body. (pages 164–167)

For further review, use Study Guide pages 232–233.

Checking Health Vocabulary

Number your paper from 1–9. Match each meaning in Column I with the correct word or words in Column II.

Column I

1. certain living things made of one cell that can cause diseases such as strep throat and tuberculosis
2. a medicine that can prevent a disease
3. a tiny germ that can cause diseases such as measles, mumps, and polio
4. a drug found in drinks such as coffee, tea, cola, and cocoa
5. a medicine that can be bought without a prescription
6. a drug that can be harmful and is found in beer, wine, and liquor
7. a drug in tobacco that can harm a smoker's heart
8. a medicine that can be bought only with a doctor's order
9. an unwanted change caused by taking a medicine

Column II

a. alcohol
b. bacteria
c. caffeine
d. nicotine
e. over-the-counter medicine
f. prescription medicine
g. side effect
h. vaccine
i. virus

Chapter 6 Test

Complete the Sentence

Number your paper from 1–10. Next to each number write the word that best completes the sentence. Choose the words from the list below.

adult	nicotine
drug	pharmacist
bacteria	prescription
labels	vaccines
medicines	viruses

1. Medicines are a kind of ____.
2. A ____ is an order for a medicine.
3. A ____ fills the order for a prescription medicine.
4. Some medicines help cure diseases by killing the ____ that cause the diseases.
5. People get ____ to prevent diseases such as measles, mumps, and polio.
6. Germs called ____ cause measles, mumps, and polio.
7. Only an ____ in charge of a child should give the child medicine.
8. Leave the ____ on medicines.
9. People should use ____ only if they really need them.
10. Caffeine, alcohol, and ____ are drugs that can harm health.

Short Answer

Number your paper from 11–17. Next to each number write the word or words that best answer the question.

11. What kind of medicines can be bought without a prescription?
12. What can some bacteria and viruses cause?
13. Who should a child tell about a side effect from medicine?
14. How can medicines be kept away from small children?
15. What might a person do for a headache besides taking medicine?
16. What substance in cigarette smoke can cause lung cancer?
17. What do all cigarette packages have written on them?

Essay

Write the answers on your paper. Use complete sentences.

18. What can people do to stay safe when using medicines?
19. What advice would you give someone who is thinking of smoking a cigarette?

Health at Home

Being Safe with Medicines at Home

Talk with your family about safe ways to use medicines at home. You and your family might want to check how medicines are stored in your home. You could also answer the following questions with your family about medicine safety.

- Are medicines stored out of the reach of small children?
- Are medicines stored in the containers they came in?
- Are the labels on medicines?
- Do medicines all have caps on them?

If your family finds problems with medicine safety, discuss what to do.

Reading at Home

The Sick of Being Sick Book by Bob Jovial Stine and Jane Stine. Dutton, 1980. Discover ways to feel better at times without taking medicine.

Tobacco: What It Is, What It Does by Judith S. Seixas. Greenwillow Books, 1981. Learn how smoking can be harmful to your health.

Chapter 7

Your Physical Fitness

This boy is working to become physically fit. You might also want to become physically fit. If so, what should you do?

The lessons in this chapter tell about ways to become physically fit. The chapter has several exercises you might do. Be sure to have your teacher help you learn to do them correctly. Being physically fit can help you stay healthy throughout your life.

physical (fiz′ə kəl) **fitness,** the ability to exercise without getting tired or injured easily.

posture (pos′chər), the way a person holds his or her body.

1 How Can Being Physically Fit Help You?

What game are these children playing? What games do you like to play? How can you have fun while you are playing?

If you have **physical fitness,** you can play and work without getting tired easily. Physical fitness can help you have more fun playing games.

Being physically fit can help you look your best. You will have stronger muscles in your back, arms, legs, and over your stomach. Strong muscles help you have good **posture.** Good posture helps you sit, stand, or walk comfortably.

Being physically fit might help prevent heart diseases. Most children do not have a problem with heart diseases. Being physically fit is still important for you. Becoming fit now might help keep you from having heart diseases later in life.

Often, being physically fit can help you do something you have wanted to do. Maybe you wanted to ride a bicycle. You practiced for a long time. How did you feel when you were able to ride your bicycle well?

Think Back • *Study on your own with Study Guide page 234.*

1. What is physical fitness?
2. How can being physically fit help a person?

agility (ə jil′ə tē), the ability to move quickly and easily.

2 How Does Having Agility Help You?

The picture shows children moving quickly and easily in different activities. They have **agility.** Agility is a part of physical fitness.

When you have agility, you can play games better. What games do you need agility to play? Some people need agility to do their jobs well. For example, people who put up telephone lines need agility.

Log roll

Cartwheel

You can do certain stunts to find out if you have agility. You can read about these stunts on page 178. Practicing these stunts can help you improve your agility. Then you can play and work better.

On Your Own
What activity is agility helping each child in the pictures do well? List the activities on your paper and write directions for each activity.

Think Back • *Study on your own with Study Guide page 234.*

1. What is agility?
2. How can having agility help when playing or working?
3. What can improve agility?

Forward roll

Backward roll

Health Activities Workshop

Finding Out About Agility

1. Try the Half Turn. Stand with your feet apart. Jump in the air as shown and turn while you are jumping. Land facing the opposite direction from which you started. Could you do this stunt easily?

2. Try the Full Turn. Stand with your feet apart. Jump in the air and turn while you are jumping. Land facing the same direction from which you started. Could you do this stunt easily?

3. Try the Heel Click. Jump in the air. Try to click your heels together. Be sure to bend your knees and click the backs of your heels together. Next, jump and try to click your heels two times. Could you click your heels two times?

Half turn

Looking at Careers

4. Do you like to look around in sports equipment stores? Do you like sports that use equipment? Then you might like to be a **sports equipment salesperson.**

One kind of sports equipment salesperson works for a factory that makes sports equipment. The salesperson visits stores that sell sports equipment. The salesperson shows the managers of the stores the sports equipment that the factory makes. The managers can buy the equipment to sell in their stores.

Many sports equipment salespeople learn about their jobs while they are working. Others learn about their jobs when they go to college.

Make a list of the equipment you would need to take part in one sport. You might check to see if the equipment is sold in any sports equipment stores.

3 How Much Exercise Do You Need?

What exercises is the girl doing? How often is she exercising?

Try to exercise several times a day to help yourself stay healthy. When could you exercise during the day? You might exercise in the morning before school starts. Walking to school can be good exercise if you walk fast. You might exercise by playing active games during recess. After school, you might exercise by running or by riding your bike.

Try to stay active for many minutes at a time when you exercise. Exercising for fifteen to thirty minutes at a time helps build physical fitness. Sometimes you might need to rest during exercise. Rest only when you need to. Exercising for at least fifteen minutes at a time is good for you.

Think Back • *Study on your own with Study Guide page 235.*

1. How often should a person exercise?
2. How long should a person exercise at a time?

On Your Own
Lisa wants to improve her physical fitness. Her friend Maria asked her to watch television after school. Her friend Glen asked her to play kickball after school. What do you think Lisa should do? Write what Lisa might say to Maria and to Glen about improving her physical fitness.

strength, being strong and able to do many different physical activities.

4 How Does Exercise Help Your Body?

The muscles in your body become weak if you do not use them. Exercising helps make your muscles strong. Strong muscles give you **strength** for many different activities.

Your body muscles are made up of many muscle cells. Notice the muscle cells in the picture. Your muscle cells get bigger when you exercise. When the cells in a muscle get bigger, the whole muscle gets bigger. Muscles are stronger when they get bigger.

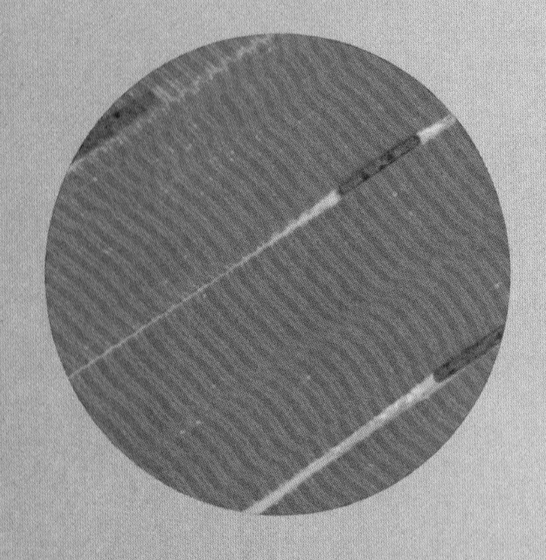

Muscle cell

You can do many different activities to make your muscles bigger and stronger. Doing yard work helps build your muscle strength. Doing exercises also helps build muscle strength. What muscles does this exercise help make strong?

Muscles that stretch easily let you bend and move easily. You can do exercises to stretch some of your muscles. Sitting on the floor and touching your toes is a good stretching exercise.

Did You Know?
Not long ago, scientists tested school children of all ages. They found that many children are not very physically fit. The tests showed that these children sit and watch television too much. The children do not get enough exercise. Some of the children decided to change. They decided to become more physically fit by walking more and sitting less.

How Does Exercise Help Your Heart and Lungs?

The girl in the picture enjoys jumping rope. She knows that this exercise will help parts of her body work better. What are these parts?

The heart is one part of the body that exercise can help work better. Your heart is a muscle. Making your heart stronger can help you stay healthy and help keep you from having heart diseases later in life. Exercise helps your heart get stronger. Your heart beats faster during exercise. When you exercise, you help make your heart stronger.

Something else happens when you exercise to strengthen your heart. Your lungs also work better. You breathe more air into your lungs as you exercise. Breathing in more air helps your lungs work better.

You make your heart and lungs work better when you exercise. What activities could you do to help your heart and lungs work better? You could ride a bicycle. You could run or go swimming.

Think Back • *Study on your own with Study Guide page 235.*

1. How does exercise make the muscles strong?
2. What can muscles that stretch easily help a person do?
3. How does exercise help the heart and lungs?

5 What Can You Do to Get Physically Fit?

Following a daily exercise plan can help you become physically fit. A good exercise plan should have exercises to make your muscles strong. It should also have exercises to make your heart and lungs work better. You might want to use the exercise plan shown on pages 188 to 193.

You should warm up your muscles before exercising, as these children are doing. You should also cool down your muscles after you exercise. Warming up and cooling down your muscles helps keep them from hurting. Stretching your muscles is a good way to warm up or cool down.

Warm up before exercising.

Follow these rules to help keep safe when you exercise.

- Choose a safe place to exercise. Be sure you have enough room to move about.
- Ask a responsible adult to show you the right way to do an exercise. Some exercises can be harmful if not done correctly.
- Wear exercise clothes that let you move freely. Keep your shoes tied. You could trip over an untied shoelace.

On Your Own
What rules are the children in the picture following to stay safe when exercising? Write the rules on your paper.

Think Back • *Study on your own with Study Guide page 235.*

1. What kinds of exercises should a good exercise plan have?
2. What can help keep muscles from being hurt during exercise?
3. What are some safety rules to follow when exercising?

project keep fit

Project Keep-Fit is an exercise program that is fun to do. Following this program every day can help you stay physically fit. Be sure to have your teacher help you learn how to do these exercises correctly. Check with your parent or guardian to find out if there is any medical reason why you should not do some of these exercises.

Warm-Up

Side Stretcher
With feet apart, reach down with one hand. Reach over your head with the other hand. Reach a little farther and hold for six to ten seconds. Repeat on other side. Do as many as you can up to three.

Leg Stretcher
Stand facing a wall about an arm's length away. Lean forward bending your arms until your elbows touch the wall. Keep your feet on the floor. Hold for six to ten seconds. Then straighten up. Do as many as you can up to three.

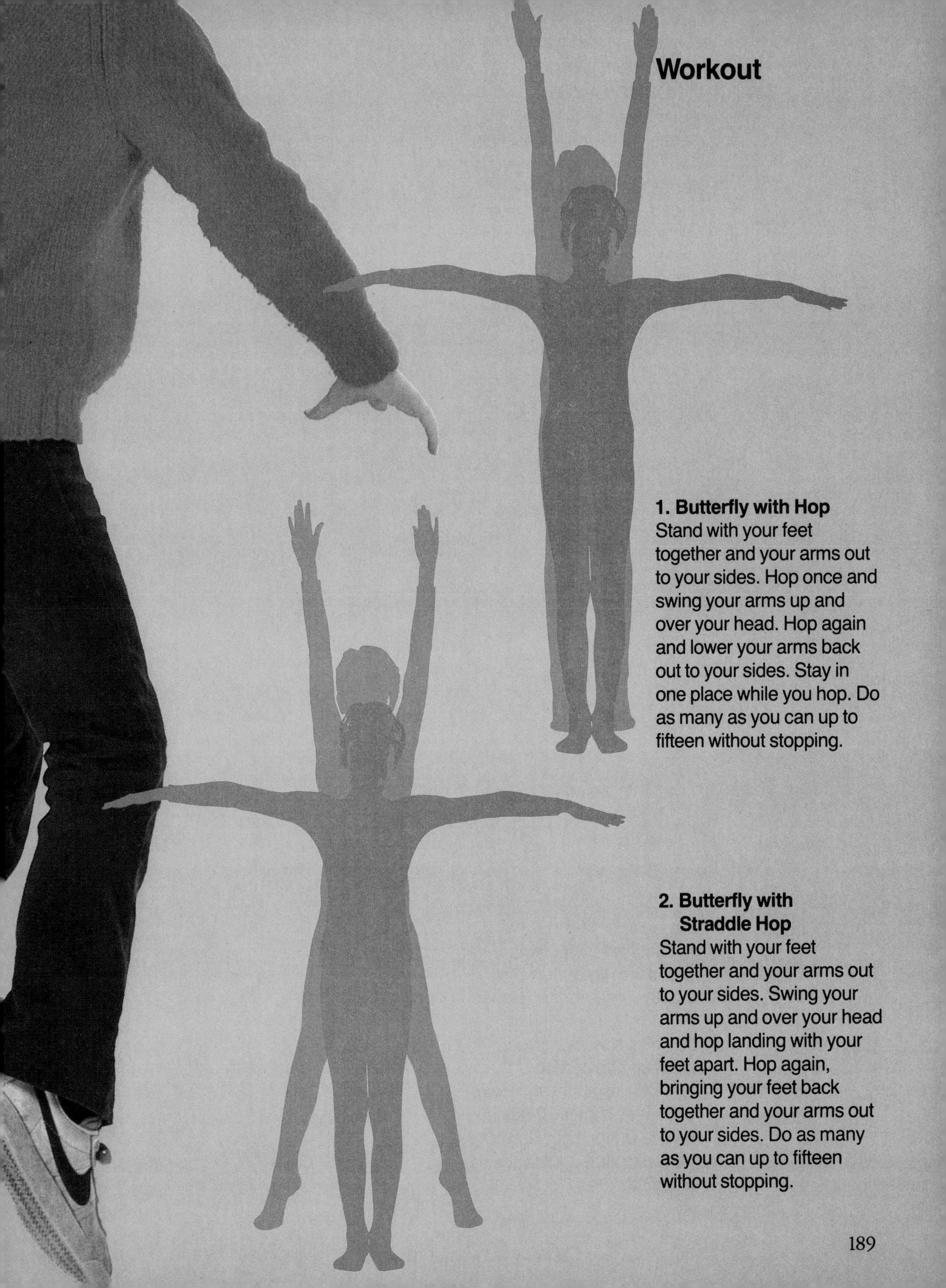

Workout

1. Butterfly with Hop
Stand with your feet together and your arms out to your sides. Hop once and swing your arms up and over your head. Hop again and lower your arms back out to your sides. Stay in one place while you hop. Do as many as you can up to fifteen without stopping.

2. Butterfly with Straddle Hop
Stand with your feet together and your arms out to your sides. Swing your arms up and over your head and hop landing with your feet apart. Hop again, bringing your feet back together and your arms out to your sides. Do as many as you can up to fifteen without stopping.

3. Butterfly with One-Foot Hop

Stand on one foot with your arms out to your sides. Hop on one foot and swing your arms up and over your head. Hop again and lower your arms back out to your sides. Try to repeat the movement on the other foot. Do as many as you can up to fifteen.

4. Jackknife with Hop

Stand with your feet together and arms stretched forward at shoulder height. Jump up and swing your arms up and over your head. Jump again and lower your arms back to shoulder height. Do as many as you can up to fifteen without stopping.

5. Jackknife with Straddle Hop

Stand with your feet together and arms stretched forward at shoulder height. Jump up, swinging your arms up and over your head. Land with your feet apart. Jump again, bringing your feet back together and your arms back to shoulder height. Do as many as you can up to fifteen without stopping.

6. Jackknife with One-Foot Hop

Stand on one foot with your arms stretched forward at shoulder height. Hop on one foot and swing your arms up and over your head. Hop again and lower your arms back to shoulder height. Try to repeat the movement on the other foot. Do as many as you can up to fifteen without stopping.

Cool-Down

Do the stretching exercises on page 188 to help prevent sore muscles.

Keeping Fit While You Play

Keep Fit While You Sit

The Twist
Sit and hold your arms out at shoulder height. Turn to the left as far as you can. Stretch your arm muscles. Next turn to the right as far as you can. Stretch your arm muscles. Hold each stretch while you count to ten. Do as many as you can up to three.

The Push and Pull
Sit with your hands together in front of you. Push your hands together as hard as you can while you count to ten. Next grip your hands and fingers and try to pull them apart while you count to ten. Do as many as you can up to three.

Tiffany Chin and Physical Fitness

Tiffany Chin is a champion ice skater. You can see in the picture the strong muscles in her legs. These strong muscles give her the strength to leap when she skates.

This young skater also needs agility to skate well. She moves quickly and easily on the ice. Because she has agility, she can dance to lively music while she skates.

Tiffany Chin practices skating about four hours every day. Practicing helped her become a great ice skater. Practicing also keeps her physically fit.

Tiffany Chin is one of the best ice skaters in the United States. She has skated in the Olympic games. She has won many medals. She hopes someday to be the best ice skater in the world.

Talk About It

1. How does practicing ice-skating help Tiffany Chin?
2. What sport could you practice to help keep yourself physically fit?

Chapter 7 Review

Reviewing Lesson Objectives

1. Tell how being physically fit can help a person. (pages 174–175)
2. Tell how having agility helps in play or work. (pages 176–177)
3. Tell how often and how long a person should exercise. (pages 180–181)
4. Tell how exercise helps the body work better. (pages 182–185)
5. Tell what kinds of exercises a good exercise plan should have. (pages 186–187)

For further review, use Study Guide pages 234-235.

Checking Health Vocabulary

Number your paper from 1–4. Match the meaning in Column I with the correct word or words in Column II.

Column I

1. being strong and able to do many different physical activities
2. the way a person holds his or her body
3. the ability to move quickly and easily
4. the ability to exercise without getting tired or injured easily

Column II

a. agility
b. physical fitness
c. posture
d. strength

Number your paper from 5–8. Next to each number write the word or words from the list below that best complete each sentence.

cool down	heart
exercise	warm up

A good (5)____ plan has exercises to make muscles strong and the (6)____ and lungs work better. It begins with a (7)____ and ends with a (8)____.

Chapter 7 Test

Choose the Best Answer

Number your paper from 1–8. Next to each number write the word that best completes the sentence. Choose the words from the list below.

agility	fit	heart
cells	fitness	safe
exercise	harmful	

1. Physical ____ can help a person play and work without getting tired easily.
2. People who have ____ move quickly and easily.
3. Try to ____ for at least fifteen minutes at a time.
4. Running, swimming, and riding a bicycle are activities that can help the ____ work better.
5. Muscle ____ get bigger when a person exercises.
6. Following a daily exercise plan can help a person become physically ____.
7. Learn the right way to do an exercise. Some exercises can be ____ if not done correctly.
8. Choose a ____ place to exercise.

Short Answer

Number your paper from 9–15. Next to each number write the word or words that best answer the question.

9. What helps a person have good posture?
10. What can a person do better if he or she has agility?
11. What might be a good exercise to do after school?
12. How does exercising help the lungs?
13. What can help stretch muscles so that a person can bend and move easily?
14. What should a person do before exercising to keep from hurting muscles?
15. What should a person do after exercising to keep from hurting muscles?

Essay

Write the answers on your paper. Use complete sentences.

16. What different ways do you build your own physical fitness each day?
17. How could improving your agility help you?

Family Fitness

You might ask some family members to exercise with you at home as this family is doing. Any family member over thirty-five might need to have a health checkup before beginning an exercise program. Maybe you could use the exercises on pages 188–193.

Different family members could take turns leading the group. The leader could tell the others what movements to do. For example, the leader might say this: "Hop five times on your left foot. One, two, three, four, five. Hop five times on your right foot. One, two, three, four, five. Now repeat."

Reading at Home

Albert the Running Bear's Exercise Book by Barbara Isenberg and Marjorie Jaffe. Clarion, 1984. Learn to do various exercises along with Albert the bear.

Body Sense, Body Nonsense by Seymour Simon. Lippincott, 1981. Find out what makes your body healthy and what does not.

Chapter 8

A Healthy Community

These children are helping keep their community healthy. What are they doing? You can help keep your community healthy too.

The lessons in this chapter tell how you can work to help keep your community healthy. You will also learn how community workers help keep a community healthy.

litter!
Keep our school clean!

On Your Own

List the places the picture shows that help people in a community stay healthy. Then add three more.

1 What Does a Healthy Community Have?

A community has many things people need to stay healthy. A community has places for people to live. It has places for people to work. It has places for people to shop for food and other things. Usually, a community has parks and other places to have fun. Which of these things do you see in this community?

People often need the help of others to stay healthy. Most communities have health workers who can give people this help. For example, doctors and dentists help people stay healthy. Nurses and hospital workers also help people stay healthy. Who are some other health workers?

Many communities have a health department. Workers in a health department help protect people from disease. Some workers help make sure that people have clean, safe food to eat. Some workers see that water is safe to drink. Other workers try to solve the problem of dirty air.

Some communities have health department **clinics.** People can get health care sometimes free or at a low cost at these places.

clinic (klin′ik), a place where people can get health care.

Think Back • *Study on your own with Study Guide page 236.*

1. What does a community have that people need to stay healthy?
2. How do health department workers help a community?

sanitarian (san′ə ter′ē ən), a person who checks to see if food is clean and safe to eat.

2 Who Helps Keep a Community's Food Safe to Eat?

People in a community need clean, safe food to eat. How is a community's food kept clean and safe?

Health workers called **sanitarians** check the food in a community. Sanitarians check to see if food is clean and safe to eat. They check the food in restaurants, food stores, dairies, and food factories.

Sanitarians report any problems they find to the community health department. The department might close a place that does not have clean and safe food to eat.

Sanitarians check food for harmful germs. Some germs that cause disease can grow in food. People might get sick if they eat food with harmful germs.

Sanitarians also check to see if food is prepared in safe ways. Some foods need to be cooked at certain temperatures to kill germs in the food. Sanitarians check to see if these foods are cooked at the right temperatures.

Sanitarians make sure that kitchens are clean. They check to see if food workers have a place to wash their hands. Washing hands with soap and water helps remove dirt and germs from hands. Workers with unclean hands might spread harmful germs to food they handle.

How are these sanitarians making sure that food is clean and safe to eat?

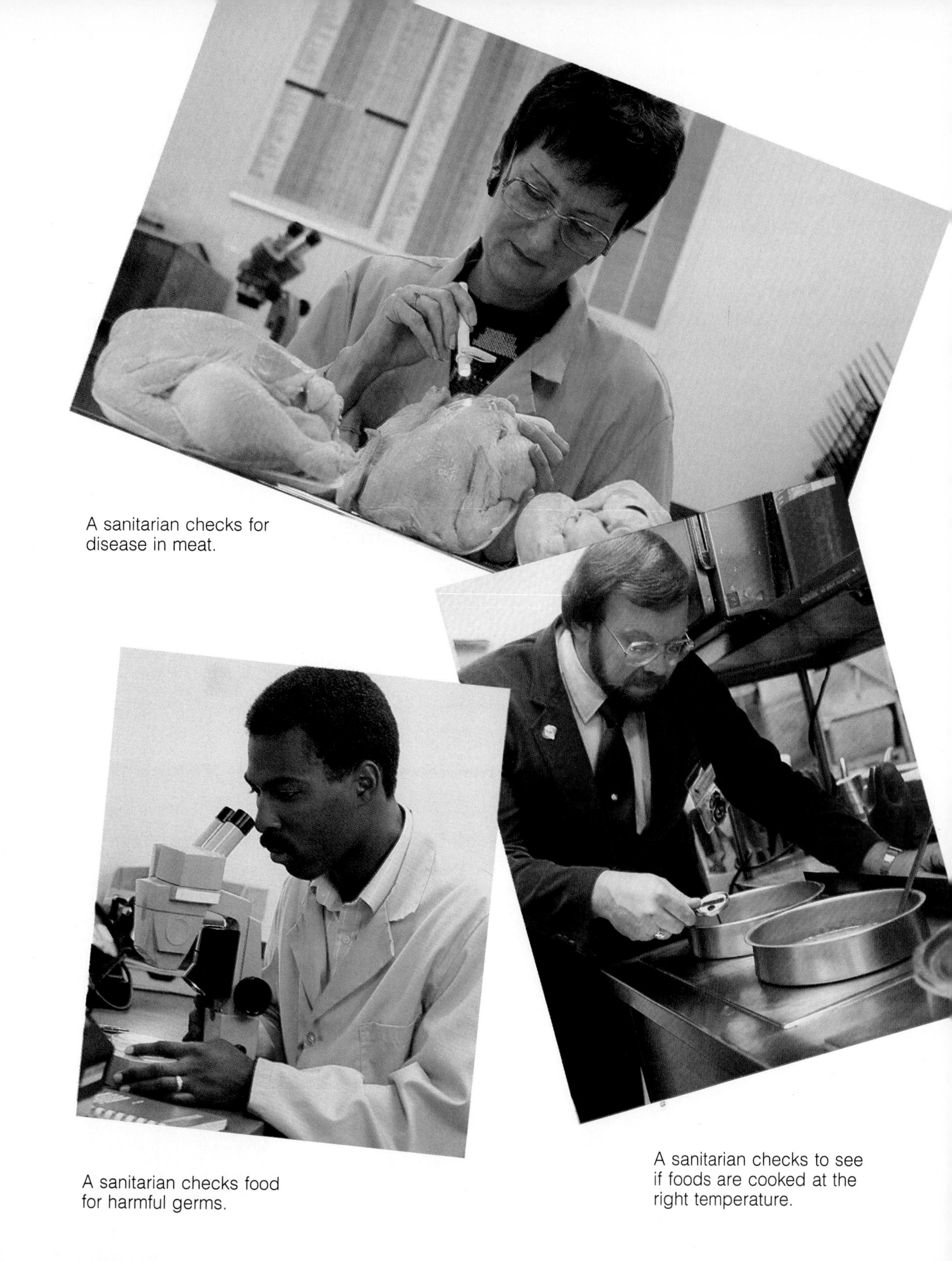

A sanitarian checks for disease in meat.

A sanitarian checks food for harmful germs.

A sanitarian checks to see if foods are cooked at the right temperature.

On Your Own
Look at the pictures in this lesson. Think about what a sanitarian does. Then pretend that you are a sanitarian checking a kitchen in a restaurant. List what you might check in the kitchen.

What Are Safe Ways to Store Food?

Sanitarians check to see if food is stored in safe ways. Storing foods safely helps keep germs from growing in them. Then people will not get sick from eating foods with harmful germs.

Storing some foods at cold temperatures helps keep them safe to eat. Germs will not grow quickly in foods that are kept cold.

Storing foods in clean containers helps keep them safe to eat. Clean containers have few harmful germs that could get into the foods.

How are these sanitarians making sure that foods are stored safely?

Think Back • *Study on your own with Study Guide page 236.*

1. How do sanitarians help keep food in a community safe to eat?
2. Why must food be prepared in safe ways?
3. Why must food be stored in safe ways?

A sanitarian checks milk containers to make sure that they are clean. What might happen to the milk if the containers are not clean?

A sanitarian checks the temperature of ground meat. The meat must be kept cold. What might happen to the meat if it is not kept cold?

A sanitarian checks the temperature of milk in a storage tank. Germs will not grow quickly in the milk if it is kept cold.

air pollution (pə lü′shən), materials in the air that are harmful to health when breathed in.

3 Who Helps Keep a Community's Air Safe to Breathe?

Some health department workers help keep a community's air clean and safe to breathe. They check for **air pollution** in the community. Air pollution is dirt and other harmful materials in the air. People can get sick from air pollution.

The workers report any air pollution they find to the health department. The health department helps the community make plans to stop the pollution.

Most air pollution comes from burning. Smoke and other harmful gases go into the air. The smoke and harmful gases make the air dirty. They **pollute** the air. Gases from fuel burned in cars and trucks cause much air pollution.

pollute (pə lüt′), to make dirty.

Some children made the picture you see here. What does the picture show about air pollution?

Think Back • *Study on your own with Study Guide page 236.*

1. Why do people need clean air to breathe?
2. How do health department workers help keep the air clean?
3. What causes air pollution?

water pollution (pə lü′shən), materials in water that are harmful to health.

4 Who Helps Keep a Community's Water Safe to Drink?

Drinking polluted water can make people sick. What can a community do to make sure its water is safe to drink?

Most communities have a water-treatment plant. Water from a river or lake first goes through pipes to the plant. Workers in the plant make the water safe to drink. Then the water is sent through smaller pipes into buildings.

Health department workers test water from the water-treatment plant. They test to see if the water is safe to drink. They report any water pollution they find to the health department. **Water pollution** is harmful materials in water. The health department makes sure the harmful materials are taken out of the water.

Health department workers also test water that people swim in. They check to see if it is safe for swimming. People can get sick from swimming in polluted water.

This health department worker tests water in a public pool. He also sends some water to a laboratory for more tests. The tests show if the water is safe for swimming.

The workers report to the health department any water pollution that they find. The department might put up a sign where water is polluted. The sign might say NO SWIMMING HERE.

What is the health department worker doing to help keep water safe for swimming?

Did You Know?
You might become very sick if you eat fish from polluted waters. For this reason, the health department puts up warning signs near polluted water. One sign might say NO FISHING HERE.

Think Back • *Study on your own with Study Guide page 237.*

1. What do many communities have to make their water safe to drink?
2. How do health department workers help keep water safe to drink?
3. How do health department workers help keep water safe to swim in?

> ***Did You Know?***
> Electricity can be made from garbage. First, garbage is burned to make heat. Then the heat boils water to make steam. The steam runs machines that make electric power. Some communities get power by burning garbage.

5 How Do Sanitation Workers Help a Community?

A clean community is a healthy place to live. Garbage and trash is picked up often in a clean community. Garbage will look and smell terrible if it is not collected often. Rats and flies can live in garbage left lying around. The rats and flies can spread harmful germs.

Sanitation workers help keep a community clean and safe. They collect garbage and trash in special trucks. Look at the pictures. What happens to the garbage and trash in different communities?

Think Back • *Study on your own with Study Guide page 237.*

1. Why should a community's garbage and trash be collected often?
2. How do sanitation workers help keep a community clean and safe?
3. Where might sanitation workers take a community's garbage and trash?

Sanitation workers collect garbage and trash that nobody wants. They load the garbage into the back of a garbage truck.

Special equipment inside the truck mashes the garbage and pushes it back into the truck.

In some communities, garbage trucks take garbage to places called landfills. The garbage is dumped there. Then bulldozers flatten it. Finally, bulldozers bury the garbage.

In some communities, garbage is taken to be burned in large furnaces called incinerators.

Health Activities Workshop

Learning More About a Community

1. Make a model of a community like the one shown. You might want to use cardboard boxes, clay, and toy objects to make your community. Show what a community has to help people stay healthy. Place your community where others can see it.

2. Find the mystery message. It tells something about pollution. Read the lines from left to right. The letters make a sentence. What is the sentence?

C A R S M A
K E M U C H
A I R P O L
L U T I O N

3. Find out where the sanitation workers in your community take the garbage they collect. You might ask your teacher or parent to help you. You could look under Garbage Collection in the yellow pages of a community telephone book. Then draw pictures to show what happens to the garbage.

Looking at Careers

4. **Public health nurses** work for a community's health department. They help care for people in a community in many different ways.

Some public health nurses visit schools and help care for children. Some go into homes and help families with health problems. A public health nurse might show a family how to care for someone who is sick. He or she might show a family how to take care of a newborn baby. What is this public health nurse doing? Write a story explaining what the nurse is doing.

Would you like to become a public health nurse? If so, you need to go to college between two and four years.

On Your Own

Write a story telling how the family in the picture is helping their community.

litter, trash that is not thrown away as it should be.

recycle (rē sī′kəl), to use something over again.

6 How Can You Help Your Community?

The people in the picture are helping their community. How are they helping?

You can help your community by not leaving any **litter** lying around. Litter is trash that is not thrown away as it should be. Litter can make a community dirty and unattractive. Litter can cause health problems. For example, a person could get cut by broken glass left in the grass. Throw away all litter correctly. Put it in a covered can or in a plastic bag that closes tightly.

You can help your community by using some things over again. For example, you can use clean paper bags more than once. Your community will have less trash to get rid of if you use things again. You **recycle** things when you use them again.

Your community might have a recycling center. You can collect cans, glass bottles, and newspapers and bring them to a center. These objects can be recycled to make new cans, bottles, and paper.

Think Back • *Study on your own with Study Guide page 237.*

1. How can not leaving litter lying around help a community?
2. How can recycling things help a community?

Health Focus

Helping the Green Bay Community

The school children in Green Bay, Wisconsin, plant trees each year to help their community. The trees help the community look beautiful. They also help the community have less air pollution.

Planting groups of trees can help make city air less polluted. The leaves on trees help take pollution out of the air. Tiny hairs on the outsides of the leaves trap bits of pollution in the air. The bits of pollution stay on the leaves until rain washes them off.

The children in Green Bay first started planting trees in 1964. The children buy young trees from the city at a low cost. They plant the trees in late spring. Since 1964, the children have planted over 60,000 trees.

Talk About It

1. How do the trees that children in Green Bay plant help keep the air clean?
2. How could you help keep the air in your community clean?

Chapter 8 Review

Reviewing Lesson Objections

1. Tell what a community has to help keep people in the community healthy. (pages 200–201)
2. Tell how sanitarians work to help keep food in a community clean and safe to eat. (pages 202–205)
3. Tell how some health department workers help keep a community's air safe to breathe. (pages 206–207)
4. Tell how some health department workers help keep a community's water safe to drink. (pages 208–209)
5. Tell how sanitation workers help keep a community clean and safe. (pages 210–211)
6. Tell what people can do to help keep themselves and their community healthy. (pages 214–215)

For further review, use Study Guide pages 236-237.

Checking Health Vocabulary

Number your paper from 1–8. Match each meaning in Column I with the correct word or words in Column II.

Column I

1. a place where people live, work, shop, and play
2. a place where people can get health care
3. a person who checks to see if food is clean and safe to eat
4. materials in the air that are harmful to health when breathed in
5. to make dirty
6. materials in water that are harmful to health
7. trash that is not thrown away as it should be
8. to use something over again

Column II

a. air pollution
b. clinic
c. community
d. litter
e. pollute
f. recycle
g. sanitarian
h. water pollution

Chapter 8 Test

Complete the Sentence

Number your paper from 1–8. Next to each number write the word that best completes the sentence. Choose the words from the list below.

air	harmful
clean	health
community	recycle
food	trash

1. Places to live, work, shop, and have fun can be found in a ____.
2. Sanitarians check to see if ____ is clean and safe to eat.
3. Gases from fuels burned in cars and trucks cause much ____ pollution.
4. At a water-treatment plant, ____ materials are taken out of water.
5. A ____ community is a healthy place to live, work, and play.
6. A community's garbage and ____ should be picked up often.
7. Litter can cause ____ problems in a community.
8. People help their community have less trash when they ____ things.

Short Answer

Number your paper from 9–15. Next to each number write the word or words that best answer the question.

9. Who works to help keep people in a community healthy?
10. What can germs in food cause?
11. How can food workers keep from spreading harmful germs to the food they handle?
12. What can the health department do about air pollution in a community?
13. What might a sign next to polluted water say?
14. How do sanitation workers help keep a community clean and safe?
15. Where should litter be placed?

Essay

Write the answers on your paper. Use complete sentences.

16. What other ways can people in a community enjoy water that is safe for swimming?
17. What could you do around the outside of your home to help your community?

Health at Home

Helping Your Community

What can you tell your family about sanitation workers? How can you and your family help these workers?

You can help the sanitation workers in your community have less trash to pick up. Recycle old clothes, books, and toys. Do not throw them out.

You could save newspapers and bring them to recycling centers. The papers can be taken to factories. Old papers get made into new papers at these factories.

You could also save glass bottles, metal cans, and plastic containers. Then bring the items to a recycling center. The items can be recycled to make new bottles, cans, and containers.

Reading at Home

Keeping Our Cities Clean by Ross R. Olney. Messner, 1979. Find out how a city is kept clean and healthy.

What Is a Community? by Caroline Arnold. Watts, 1982. Discover what different communities are like.

Acknowledgments (Picture Credits)

Page 34: Ben Weaver/Camera 5
Page 62: Courtesy Parke-Davis, Division of Warner-Lambert Company
Pages 68, 69: Ed Reschke (all)
Page 88: Bettmann Archive
Page 102: Courtesy Naval Dental Research Institute
Pages 103, 105: Copyright by the American Dental Association. Reprinted by permission.
Page 116: Courtesy *M.D. Magazine,* October 1974
Page 154 (l): © 1985 Martin M. Rotker/Taurus
Page 155 (c): Michael Abbey/Photo Researchers
(r): © 1984 Martin M. Rotker/Taurus
Page 156 (l, c): Centers for Disease Control, Atlanta, GA. 30333
(r): Omicron/Photo Researchers Inc.
Page 168: Wide World Photos, Inc.
Page 182 (t): Ed Reschke
Page 194: Focus on Sports, Inc.

All photographs not credited are the property of Scott, Foresman and Company. These include photographs taken by the following photographer:

James L. Ballard: Pages 16–17, 18–19, 21, 22–23, 24–25, 26–27, 28, 29, 31, 32–33, 37, 38–39, 40–41, 42–43, 44–45, 48–49, 50, 51, 52–53, 54, 55, 58, 61, 65, 66–67, 73, 75, 78, 79, 84, 85, 86–87, 91, 92–93, 97, 106, 107, 108, 110, 111, 114, 115, 119, 120–121, 122–123, 124, 125, 126–127, 128–129, 132–133, 134, 135, 136, 137, 141, 142, 143, 147, 148–149, 151, 157, 159, 161, 162, 163, 164–165, 167, 171, 172–173, 175, 176–177, 178, 179, 180–181, 182–183, 185, 186–187, 188–189, 190–191, 192–193, 197, 198–199, 203, 204–205, 208–209, 210, 211, 212, 213, 215, 216, 219

Independent Study Guide

Use the *Independent Study Guide* to review the lessons in each chapter. After you read each lesson, answer the questions to find out what you remember. Answering the questions will help you learn the important ideas in each lesson. You can also use the study guide to help you review for the chapter test.

Chapter 1 Study Guide

On a separate sheet of paper, write the word or words that best complete the sentence or answer the question.

Lesson **1** pages 18-19

1. Happiness, sadness, anger, worry, and surprise are ____.
2. What might a person's face show who feels happy?
3. Listening to a person's ____ is one way to tell how he or she feels.
4. People can show their feelings in the way they ____ or move.

Lesson **2** pages 20-21

1. A person might have scared feelings when he or she starts to learn ____ things.
2. What kind of feelings might a person have who is afraid of not doing something well?
3. Sometimes talking about scared feelings helps a person feel ____.
4. Who might a scared person talk with to feel less scared?

Lesson **3** pages 22-23

1. A ____ might give advice on how to change hurt feelings.
2. How can saying the words "I'm sorry" help when a person has hurt someone else's feelings?
3. A person who often does unkind things to others must act ____ to keep from hurting others' feelings.

Lesson **4** pages 24-25

1. Who might a sad person talk with to help himself or herself feel better?
2. Family members often know that a person whose pet has died feels very ____.
3. Family members might suggest ____ to help a sad person feel better.
4. Going ahead and crying often helps a sad person feel ____.

Lesson **5** pages 26-27

1. A person might feel ____ when things go wrong.
2. What active things might a child who feels angry do outside to feel better?
3. An angry person might do something for ____ to help himself or herself feel better.
4. Who might an angry child ask for some work to do to help himself or herself feel better?

Lesson **6** pages 30-33

1. Too much arguing can ____ people.
2. What can help people get along better with others and argue less?
3. A person who shows ____ does his or her best to work with other people.
4. What can family members do around the home to show cooperation?
5. What are children showing toward a newcomer when they ask him or her to join their game?
6. A person shows ____ when he or she tries to think of how another person feels?
7. What might a person say to someone who has made a mistake to show understanding?

Chapter 2 Study Guide

On a separate sheet of paper, write the word or words that best complete the sentence or answer the question.

Lesson 1
pages 40-43

1. What plan can be used to help choose healthy foods?
2. The four food group plan tells the number of daily ____ needed from each food group.
3. What are three ways that nutrients help the body?
4. The ____ in different foods work together to help the body stay healthy.

Lesson 2
pages 44-47

1. What kinds of foods make up a healthy meal?
2. Two servings are needed each day from the ____ group.
3. Three servings are needed each day from the ____ group.
4. Four servings are needed each day from both the bread-cereal and the ____ group.

Lesson 3
pages 48-49

1. A person needs to eat ____ kinds of vegetables.
2. Different kinds of vegetables give the body different kinds of ____.
3. The ____ needs the different kinds of nutrients in vegetables to stay healthy.
4. What ways other than fresh can vegetables be bought?

Lesson
4
pages
52-54

1. Healthy snacks should not be too ___ or salty.
2. Sweet snacks can stick to the ___ and harm them.
3. What are three healthy drinks?
4. Many foods eaten at meals contain salt so ___ salt should not be added to the foods.
5. Milk, cheese, and yogurt are healthy snacks from the ___ group.
6. What are some healthy snacks from the vegetable-fruit group?

Lesson
5
pages
56-57

1. A person needs to read the labels on cans to be a ___ food shopper.
2. A wise food shopper can find out which kind of food will cost the least by looking at ___.
3. What should a wise food shopper be willing to try?
4. The best tasting foods do not always ___ the most.

Lesson
6
pages
60-61

1. What should you wash your hands with before handling foods?
2. What is removed from hands when they are washed?
3. What is removed from fresh fruits and vegetables when they are washed?
4. Some leftover foods should be put in a ___.
5. Germs can grow in certain foods that get ___.
6. Germs do not grow as quickly in ___ places as they do in warm.

Chapter 3 Study Guide

On a separate sheet of paper, write the word or words that best complete the sentence or answer the question.

Lesson 1
pages 68-69

1. Bones, ____, nerves, and blood make up the inside of the body.
2. The smallest living parts of the body are ____.
3. Each kind of cell does a ____ job.
4. Cells of the same kind that are grouped together make up ____.
5. What kind of tissue do many bone cells together make up?

Lesson 2
pages 70-72

1. What are the muscles in the body attached to?
2. The muscles in the body work in ____.
3. Under the muscles in the body are ____.
4. What makes up a body's skeleton?
5. What body parts help a person move about?
6. What joint lets a person swing a bat?

Lesson 3
pages 74-75

1. The brain is an ____ made up of different kinds of tissues.
2. A person's ____ sends messages to the muscles about how to move.
3. Nerves are not all the ____ size.
4. Where are nerves found in the body?
5. The five senses are sight, ____, taste, hearing, and touch.

Lesson **4** pages 76-77

1. About how many times a minute does a child's heart beat?
2. What kind of tissue makes up most of the heart?
3. Blood carries oxygen and ___ to body cells.
4. What gas do body cells need to stay alive?
5. Blood picks up carbon dioxide and other ___ from body cells.
6. Blood travels to all parts of the body through little tubes called ___ vessels.

Lesson **5** pages 78-79

1. Where are the lungs found in the body?
2. Where does air breathed into the body through the nose or mouth go?
3. The heart pumps blood to the ___ where the blood picks up oxygen for body cells.
4. What gas is breathed out of the body?

Lesson **6** pages 80-83

1. When the body ___ food, it changes the form of the food.
2. Food is mixed with saliva so it can be ___.
3. What helps move food along the food tube?
4. Nutrients enter the blood through blood vessels in the ___ intestine.
5. Wastes leave the body through the ___ intestine.

Lesson **7** pages 86-87

1. Cells ___ to form new cells.
2. Your body becomes ___ as it adds new cells.
3. Each person grows in a way that is ___ for him or her.
4. Exercise helps ___ grow larger and stronger.
5. How does sleep help the body?

Chapter 4 Study Guide

On a separate sheet of paper, write the word or words that best complete the sentence or answer the question.

Lesson **1** pages 94-96

1. The hard, white material that helps protect the crown is called ____.
2. The ____ of a tooth are under the gum.
3. The center of a tooth has ____ and blood vessels.
4. What two things does blood carry to the teeth?
5. The blood carries ____ away from the teeth.
6. The nerves in a tooth send messages from the tooth to the ____.

Lesson **2** pages 98-101

1. How many primary teeth will a baby have by age three?
2. Primary teeth help ____ a person's face.
3. What can help keep primary teeth from coming out too soon?
4. What kind of tooth replaces a lost primary tooth?
5. If a permanent tooth does not have enough room, it may grow in ____.
6. What can hold a space open for a permanent tooth that will grow in later?

Lesson **3** pages 102-103

1. Plaque is a sticky covering of harmful ____.
2. What are two places where plaque forms?
3. The germs in plaque use ____ to make an acid that can harm teeth.
4. A hole in a tooth is called a ____.
5. Plaque can hurt ____ as well as teeth.

Lesson **4** pages 104-109

1. Brushing teeth helps prevent ___.
2. How many times a day should teeth be brushed?
3. Brushing helps remove ___ and bits of food from the teeth and gums.
4. What can remove bits of food from between the teeth and near the gum line?
5. Dental floss should be gently moved up and down the ___ of a tooth.
6. Eating foods from the four food groups each day will help keep teeth and ___ healthy.
7. Try not to eat too many ___, sticky foods.
8. Sugar can stick to ___ and cause cavities.
9. Who uses special tools to clean plaque off teeth?
10. Even if you brush and floss your teeth, some ___ might stay on the teeth and harden.
11. Plaque can cause ___ disease.

Lesson **5** pages 112-115

1. What might an advertisement tell about a product?
2. What special seal should a person look for on a tube of toothpaste?
3. The ADA puts its seal on toothpastes that help ___ cavities.
4. Use a toothbrush that is the right ___ for your mouth.
5. A toothbrush should be flat on the top with soft, ___ edges.
6. You might find ___ dental floss easier to use if your teeth are close together.

Chapter 5 Study Guide

On a separate sheet of paper, write the word or words that best complete the sentence or answer the question.

Lesson 1 pages 121-123

1. What directions should you remember to look when crossing a street?
2. Each person is most responsible for his or her ___ safety.
3. Following ___ rules can help keep you safe.
4. Thinking of ways to ___ an accident can help keep you safe.

Lesson 2 pages 124-125

1. Locked car doors prevent people from ___ out of a car accidentally.
2. What should you wear when riding in a car?
3. Never bother the ___ of a car.

Lesson 3 pages 126-127

1. An adult should help a child ___ a bicycle to see if it is safe to drive.
2. Name four things needed on a bicycle to help keep a driver safe.
3. A bicycle driver should use ___ signals when turning.

Lesson 4 pages 128-129

1. When unplugging a toaster, never pull on the ___.
2. Never touch small electric appliances with ___ hands.
3. What kinds of injuries can electricity cause?

Lesson 5
pages 130-131

1. Some cleaning products contain ____ that can be harmful.
2. Many products need to be used only in rooms with lots of ____ air.
3. What kinds of products should be stored away from food?

Lesson 6
pages 132-133

1. What should a swimmer do after reading a warning sign?
2. When should a swimmer call for help?
3. A swimmer should come out of the water if he or she feels ____ or cold.

Lesson 7
pages 136-139

1. What can be put in a home to warn of fire?
2. What can help keep a person from breathing in gases and smoke from a fire?
3. What should a person do if his or her clothes catch on fire?
4. Once a person gets out of a ____ home, he or she should not go back in for any reason.
5. A person whose home is on fire should ____ the fire department from a neighbor's home.

Lesson 8
pages 140-144

1. Try to get ____ help if someone is injured.
2. Who will help a person if he or she dials the number 0 on a telephone?
3. Listen to any ____ that are given when telephoning for help.
4. What should a small cut be washed with?
5. Press ____ on the bandage over a small cut if it keeps bleeding.
6. Run ____ water over an insect bite.

Chapter 6 Study Guide

On a separate sheet of paper, write the word or words that best complete the sentence or answer the question.

Lesson 1
pages 150-153

1. Medicines are a kind of ____.
2. Drugs can change how a person thinks, ____, or acts.
3. What kind of medicine do people need a doctor's order to buy?
4. Who fills the order for a prescription medicine?
5. What can be found on the label of a prescription medicine?
6. People do not need a prescription to buy ____ medicines.

Lesson 2
pages 154-157

1. Some medicines help cure diseases by killing ____ that cause the diseases.
2. What are some places where germs can be found?
3. Germs must get ____ the body to cause disease.
4. Germs can get into the ____ when a person breathes.
5. When germs upset the way the body works, a person becomes ____.
6. ____ cause strep throat and tuberculosis.
7. ____ called viruses can cause measles, mumps, and polio.
8. Virusus are much ____ than bacteria.
9. Medicine might help lessen the ____ of a broken bone.

Lesson **3** pages 158-159

1. Medicines can ____ people if used the wrong way.
2. Prescription medicines should never be ____ with someone else.
3. An upset stomach or a headache could be a ____ effect from a medicine.
4. Where should medicines be stored to keep them away from small children?
5. Leave the ____ on all medicines so people can read them.
6. Most small children cannot open medicines with ____ caps.

Lesson **4** pages 160-161

1. What might a person do to help make a headache feel better other than taking medicine?
2. A person does not need to take ____ for every tiny ache or pain.
3. When you are upset, ____ might help you feel better.
4. Who should help a child decide if he or she needs a medicine to feel better?

Lesson **5** pages 164-167

1. Drinks that contain certain ____ are not healthy.
2. What are four drinks that contain caffeine?
3. What affect does caffeine have on the heart?
4. Too much caffeine causes some people to feel nervous or to lose ____.
5. Alcohol changes the way a person's ____ works.
6. The nicotine in a cigarette makes it ____ for a smoker to stop smoking.
7. What drug in cigarettes can cause heart disease?
8. What kind of warning is found on a cigarette package?

Chapter 7 Study Guide

On a separate sheet of paper, write the word or words that best complete the sentence or answer the question.

Lesson **1** pages 174-175

1. Physical fitness can help a person have more ___ playing games.
2. What can help a person work or play without getting tired easily?
3. Being physically fit can help you ___ your best.
4. A physically fit person has strong back, arm, ___, and stomach muscles.
5. Strong muscles help a person have good ___.
6. What can a person do comfortably if he or she has good posture?
7. Being physically fit might help prevent a child from having ___ diseases later in life.

Lesson **2** pages 176-177

1. People need ___ to move quickly and easily.
2. Agility is a part of physical ___.
3. What is a job that a person needs agility to do well?
4. Practicing certain stunts can help a person ___ his or her agility.

Lesson **3** pages 180-181

1. Try to ___ several times a day to stay healthy.
2. Walking to school can be good exercise if you walk ___.
3. At recess play ___ games to get exercise.
4. What are two exercises that a child might do after school?
5. Exercise at least fifteen to ___ minutes at a time.
6. You might need to ___ during exercise.

Lesson **4** pages 182-185

1. What happens to muscles in the body if they are not used?
2. Exercising helps make muscles ____.
3. Body muscles are made up of many muscle ____.
4. Muscle cells get ____ when a person exercises.
5. What is a good stretching exercise?
6. Muscles that stretch easily let you ____ and move easily.
7. What can a person do to help his or her heart work better?
8. The heart beats ____ during exercise.
9. Exercises that strengthen the heart also help the ____ work better.
10. What activities can you do to help your heart and lungs work better?

Lesson **5** pages 186-187

1. A good exercise plan should have exercises to make ____ strong.
2. A good exercise plan should have exercises to make the ____ and lungs work better.
3. Why should muscles be warmed up before exercising?
4. When should a person cool down his or her muscles?
5. A good way to warm up or cool down is by ____ your muscles.
6. Choose a ____ place to exercise.
7. Who should show a child the right way to do an exercise?
8. An exercise can be ____ if not done correctly.
9. Wear exercise clothes that let you move ____.

Chapter 8 Study Guide

On a separate sheet of paper, write the word or words that best complete the sentence or answer the question.

Lesson **1** pages 200-201

1. What has places for people to live, work, shop, and have fun?
2. Doctors, ____, nurses, and hospital workers help people stay healthy.
3. Many communities have a ____ department.
4. Workers in a health department help protect people from ____.
5. People can get health care at a ____.

Lesson **2** pages 202-205

1. What are four places where sanitarians check to see if food is clean and safe to eat?
2. What might the health department do about a place that does not have clean and safe food?
3. People might get ____ if they eat food with harmful germs.
4. What might workers with unclean hands spread to the food they handle?
5. Store some foods at ____ temperatures to help keep germs from growing quickly in them.
6. Storing food safely keeps ____ from growing.

Lesson **3** pages 206-207

1. People can get ____ from air pollution.
2. Who can help a community make plans to stop air pollution?
3. Most air pollution comes from ____.
4. Smoke and harmful gases ____ the air.

Lesson **4** pages 208-209

1. Drinking ___ water can make people sick.
2. Most communities have a ___ plant to make water safe to drink.
3. Water from a river or lake goes through ___ to a water-treatment plant.
4. Who tests water from a water-treatment plant to see if it is safe to drink?
5. What is water pollution?

Lesson **5** pages 210-211

1. What two things are picked up often to help keep a community clean?
2. Garbage will look and ___ terrible if it is not collected often.
3. Rats and ___ can spread harmful germs.
4. Sanitation workers collect garbage and trash in ___.

Lesson **6** pages 214-215

1. Do not leave ___ lying around your community.
2. Litter can make a community ___ and unattractive.
3. Litter can cause ___ problems.
4. Throw away litter in a ___ can or in a plastic bag.
5. There will be ___ trash to get rid of if you use things over again.
6. When you use things like paperbags over again, you ___ them.
7. Recycling helps make a ___ and safer community.
8. What are some objects that you might collect and bring to a recycling center?

Glossary

Glossary

Pronunciation Key

The pronunciation of each word is shown just after the word, in this way: **ab bre vi ate** (ə brē′vē āt). The letters and signs used are pronounced as in the words below. The mark ′ is placed after a syllable with primary or heavy accent, as in the example above. The mark ′ after a syllable shows a secondary or lighter accent, as in **ab bre vi a tion** (ə brē′vē ā′shən).

a	hat, cap
ā	age, face
ä	father, far
b	bad, rob
ch	child, much
d	did, red
e	let, best
ē	equal, be
ėr	term, learn
f	fat, if
g	go, bag
h	he, how
i	it, pin
ī	ice, five
j	jam, enjoy
k	kind, seek
l	land, coal
m	me, am
n	no, in
ng	long, bring
o	hot, rock
ō	open, go
ô	order, all
oi	oil, voice
ou	house, out
p	paper, cup
r	run, try
s	say, yes
sh	she, rush
t	tell, it
th	thin, both
ꟛH	then, smooth
u	cup, butter
u̇	full, put
ü	rule, move
v	very, save
w	will, woman
y	young, yet
z	zero, breeze
zh	measure, seizure

ə represents:
- **a** in about
- **e** in taken
- **i** in pencil
- **o** in lemon
- **u** in circus

A

accident (ak′sə dənt), unexpected event that could harm someone.

agility (ə jil′ə tē), the ability to move quickly and easily.

alcohol (al′kə hôl), a drug that can be harmful and is found in beer, wine, and liquor.

air pollution (pə lü′shən), materials in the air that are harmful to health when breathed in.

appliance (ə plī′əns), a machine used to do a certain job.

argue (är′gyü), give reasons for or against something.

argument (är′gyə mənt), discussion by persons who do not agree.

artist (är′tist), a person who paints pictures.

B

bacteria (bak tir′ē ə), certain living things made of one cell that can cause diseases such as strep throat and tuberculosis.

blood vessel (ves′əl), a tube through which blood travels in the body.

bread-cereal group, the food group that has grains and foods made from grains.

C

caffeine (kaf′ēn), a drug found in drinks such as coffee, tea, cola, and cocoa. Too much caffeine might harm the body.

carbon dioxide (kär′bən dī ok′sīd), a colorless waste gas given off by the cells.

cavity (kav′ə tē), a hole in a tooth caused by acid.

cell (sel), the smallest living part of the body.

clinic (klin′ik), a place where people can get health care.

consideration (kən sid′ə rā′shən), thinking about another person's feelings.

cooperation (kō op′ə rā′shən), working together with other people.

crown (kroun), the part of a tooth above the gum.

D

dental floss (den′tl flos), strong thread that can help clean between the teeth.

dental hygienist (hī jē′nist), a person who helps a dentist and cleans and X-rays teeth.

dietitian (dī′ə tish′ən), a person who plans daily meals that have the right number of servings from each food group.

digest (də jest′), change food to a form that the cells in the body can use.

disease (də zēz′), an illness.

drug (drug), a substance used to treat, prevent, or cure disease.

E

electric shock, an injury caused by electricity moving through the body.

enamel (i nam′əl), the hard outer covering that protects a tooth.

F

feelings, the way a person feels about something.

first aid, immediate care given for an injury.

I-J

injury (in′jər ē), damage to the body.

joint (joint), a place where bones fit together; different joints allow different kinds of movement.

L

litter, trash that is not thrown away as it should be.

large intestine (in tes′tən), the organ of the body where wastes are passed out of the body.

M

meat-poultry-fish-bean group, the food group that has meats, poultry, fish, nuts, eggs, and beans.

milk-cheese group, the food group that has milk and foods made from milk.

N

nicotine (nik′ə tēn′), a drug in tobacco that can harm a smoker's heart.

nutrient (nü′trē ənt), a substance from food that is needed for health and growth.

O

organ (ôr′gən), a group of different tissues that work together to do the same job.

over-the-counter medicine, a medicine that can be bought without a prescription.

oxygen (ok′sə jən), a colorless gas cells take in to stay alive.

P

pasteurize (pas′chə rīz′), heat to a high enough temperature and for a long enough time to kill harmful germs.

permanent (pėr′mə nənt) **teeth**, the second set of teeth.

pharmacist (fär′mə sist), a person who fills a doctor's order for a prescription medicine.

pharmacy assistant (fär′mə sē ə sis′tənt), a person who helps a pharmacist fill orders for prescription medicines.

physical (fiz′ə kəl) **fitness**, the ability to exercise without getting tired or injured easily.

plaque (plak), a sticky material made up of germs.

poison (poi′zn), a substance that if taken into or put on the body can be dangerous to life or health.

pollute (pə lüt′), to make dirty.

posture (pos′chər), the way a person holds his or her body.

prescription (pri skrip′shən), a written direction or order for preparing and using a medicine.

prescription (pri skrip′shən) **medicine**, a medicine that can be bought only with a doctor's order.

primary (prī′mer′ē) **teeth**, first twenty teeth that come through a child's gums.

R

recycle (rē sī′kəl), to use something over again.

S-T

saliva (sə lī′və), a juice in the mouth that helps soften food.

sanitarian (san′ə ter′ē ən), a person who checks to see if food is clean and safe to eat.

sense, sight, hearing, smell, taste, or touch.

sharing, using something together.

side effect, an unwanted change caused by taking a medicine.

small intestine (in tes′tən), the organ of the body where nutrients in food enter the blood.

strength, being strong and able to do many different physical activities.

tissue (tish′ü), a group of cells that look alike.

U-V

understanding, knowing what another person is feeling.

vaccine (vak′sēn′), a medicine that can prevent a disease.

vegetable-fruit group, the food group that has vegetables and fruits.

virus (vī′rəs), a tiny germ that can cause diseases such as measles, mumps, and polio.

W-X

water pollution (pə lü′shən), materials in water that are harmful to health.

X-ray technologist (tek nol′ə jist), a person who uses an X-ray machine to take pictures of parts inside the body.

Index

Index

*A **bold-faced** number indicates a page with a picture about the topic.*

A

B

C

D

E

F

G

M

N

O

P

R

S

T

U

V

W

X

Using Metric

Metric Measures	Customary Measures

LENGTH

10 millimeters (mm) = 1 centimeter (cm)
100 centimeters = 1 meter (m)
1000 meters = 1 kilometer (km)

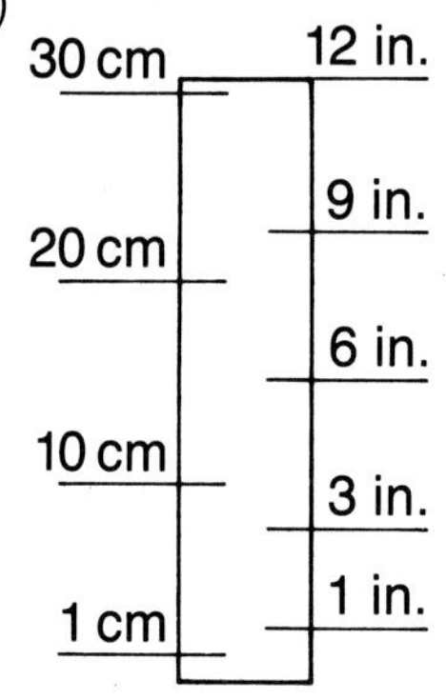

12 inches (in.) = 1 foot (ft.)
3 feet = 1 yard (yd.)
5280 feet = 1 mile (mi.)

MASS (WEIGHT)

1000 milligrams (mg) = 1 gram (g)
1000 grams = 1 kilogram (kg)
1000 kilograms = 1 metric ton (t)

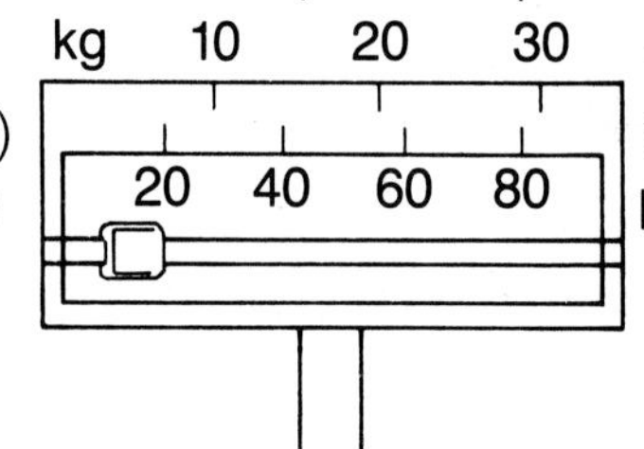

16 ounces (oz.) = 1 pound (lb.)
2000 pounds = 1 ton (t.)

VOLUME

1000 milliliters (mL) = 1 liter (l)
1000 liters = 1 kiloliter (kl)

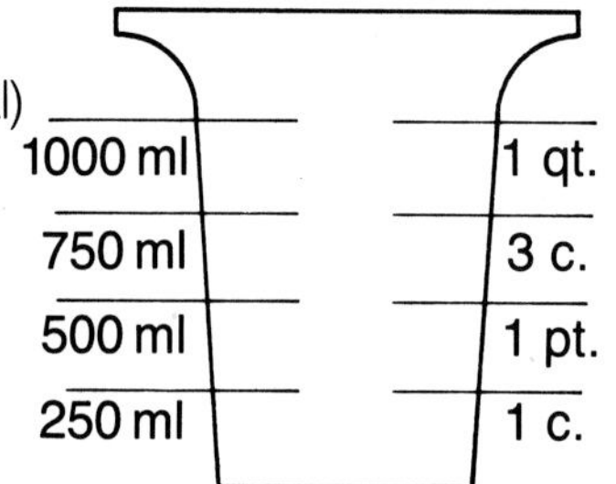

8 fluid ounces (fl. oz.) = 1 cup (c.)
2 cups = 1 pint (pt.)
2 pints = 1 quart (qt.)
4 quarts = 1 gallon (gal.)

TEMPERATURE

CELSIUS	FAHRENHEIT
Water boils 100°	212° Water boils
Body temperature 37°	98.6° Body temperature
Water freezes 0°	32° Water freezes